NO HUGS FOR HOMECOMING

BURKS PLUMMA

No Hugs for Homecoming

Copyright © [2024] by Burks Plumma

Published by [Burks Plumma Company]

ISBN: [979-8-218-52873-7]

This book chronicles my four-year journey from 2018 to 2021, as I traveled across Africa in a race against time. With genocide looming over Black Americans—disguised by white supremacy through mass immigration and gentrification—Ghana's Year of Return offered a glimmer of hope, but it also raised crucial questions. Was Africa the safe haven it promised to be, or did it hold hidden dangers? From the wealthiest elites to the poorest communities, I sought answers. Could the continent truly offer refuge for the Black diaspora, or was it a Trojan horse hiding a larger scheme to erase Black Americans for good? Each step of this urgent expedition revealed more, pushing me closer to discovering whether Africa holds the key to our survival or the final seal of our fate.

Thank you to all the Black Americans who have shared their stories with me over the years about their harrowing experiences living in Africa. Writing this memoir has been one of the hardest things I've ever done—forcing me to relive the painful memories I've carried with me every single day. But I couldn't stay silent. Too many lives are at stake, and turning a blind eye to the truth would have been a disservice to every Black person in the diaspora who has suffered in silence. Hearing the countless heartbreaking stories and witnessing the struggles firsthand, I felt a deep responsibility to speak up. Not telling the truth, after all I've seen and heard, would have been criminal. This memoir isn't just my story—it's a call to protect those who are still searching for the answers I was once seeking.

The Decision

Before I left for Africa, the weight of my decision felt crushing. It was 2018, and the world around me seemed to be closing in. The American dream, once held up as a beacon of hope, had curdled into something bitter and hollow. White supremacy was tightening its grip through mass immigration, gentrification, and systemic oppression, and every day felt like a battle for survival. The dream wasn't just slipping away—it was being ripped from our hands.

The national conversation on race was growing louder, but that's all it was—talk. Real change, the kind that could alter the course of an entire people, felt like a distant fantasy. Headlines screamed about progress, but on the ground, we were still suffocating, trapped in the same cycles of violence, poverty, and systemic neglect. For me, this wasn't just about my own struggle, it was about the survival of Black America as a whole.

That's when Ghana's 'Year of Return' broke through the noise. It wasn't just an invitation—it felt like a lifeline, a call to return to the land that birthed us, a place where we could finally escape the oppression that had defined our existence for centuries. Fueled by both determination and uncertainty, I began preparing for the journey, reaching out to a friend from Ghana who then connected me with some of their relatives to ease my arrival and smooth the introduction

However, as I dove deeper into the process—facing visa applications, fees, and endless bureaucratic hurdles—doubts began to creep in. How could a 'homecoming' feel so transactional? With each step forward, my idealized vision of Africa began to crack. Despite this, I pushed those concerns aside, reminding myself that this journey wasn't just for me; it was for all of us. Yet, beneath it all, a nagging question lingered: What if Africa wasn't the refuge I had imagined? What if, instead of offering salvation, it presented just another illusion?

This was no longer just a trip—it was a crossroads. And the weight of that question would stay with me long after my feet touched African soil.

ACCRA / EASTER REGION, GHANA

Arrival

My arrival in Accra was a true baptism by fire. As I stepped off the plane into the humid embrace of Kotoka International Airport, the bustling energy of Ghana's gateway surrounded me. A mix of excitement and nerves coursed through me, creating an intoxicating rush of anticipation for the new life ahead.

At the gate, I was warmly greeted by Hetty and Ama, relatives of a friend from the States, who had come to help me navigate my first steps in this vibrant city. Their welcoming smiles and comforting presence were a calming presence against the overwhelming sense of newness. With them by my side, the chaotic pulse of the airport seemed less intimidating, and my spirits lifted with the promise of adventure.

However, our reunion was quickly overshadowed by a sharp introduction to the challenges of local life. We had barely left the airport when a heated argument erupted with our taxi driver over the fare. The dispute escalated rapidly—words flew, tempers flared, and suddenly the situation took a dramatic turn. In a moment of anger, the driver stopped abruptly, kicked us out of the taxi, and sped off, leaving us stranded with my bags piled on the curb in a cloud of exhaust.

With no taxi in sight and limited options, Hetty, Ama, and I were forced to continue on foot. Carrying my luggage, we navigated the streets of Accra, the city's vibrant chaos now the scene to our unexpected journey. This walk became more than just a physical trek; it was a deep dive into the realities of my new environment. Hetty and Ama shared insights and advice, pointing out landmarks and local nuances as we made our way through the bustling streets.

This unexpected stroll through Accra revealed the difficulties of life here. The warmth of my initial welcome was completely different from the sudden roadside conflict, showing the unpredictable nature of my new surroundings. Despite these early challenges, Hetty and Ama's resilience and quick thinking reassured me. Their handling of the situation not only saved our plans but also showed how valuable their support was to me.

As we continued walking, the streets of Accra came alive—a vibrant mix of color, sound, and activity, full of both opportunities and potential risks. This journey, which began with a stumble, marked the start of a deeper dive into the heart of Ghanaian life, with lessons I was eager to learn and experiences I was ready to embrace.

Eventually, Hetty and Ama guided me through the bustling crowds to Kojo's house, a peaceful retreat in the heart of the city. Kojo, another relative they had arranged for me to stay with, greeted us with a warm smile and a calming presence. He quickly became my anchor in this vibrant yet overwhelming urban landscape. His home offered a temporary refuge, a place where I could regroup and plan my next steps in this dynamic new environment.

First Lessons

Living with Kojo not only provided me with shelter but also offered an invaluable introduction to the intricacies of daily life in Ghana. Each day brought new lessons in adaptation and survival as Kojo took it upon himself to guide me through his world. We ventured daily into the heart of Accra, navigating crowded markets and winding streets, where my American accent immediately caught the attention of vendors. Transactions weren't just about exchanging money—they were careful exercises in bargaining. "They hear your accent and see your wallet," Kojo would joke, though his tone carried an underlying seriousness.

It was a startling realization that here, the concept of 'blackness' was not a single identity, but but was fragmented across tribes and families, vastly different from the racial solidarity I had known or expected. This fragmentation extended into every interaction, complicating the simple notion of returning to a homeland with open arms.

Kojo was thorough in teaching me the do's and don'ts of navigating Ghana's complex social and economic landscape. His guidance became my compass as I learned to distinguish genuine help from exploitation—a vital skill in the bustling, yet unforgiving marketplace.

Our explorations extended beyond the markets. Kojo introduced me to local restaurants, where the flavors of Ghana burst forth in dishes rich with spice and history. Each meal was an opportunity to connect with locals, understand their perspectives, and further immerse myself in the cultural pulse of Accra.

One particularly memorable day, Kojo took me to the University of Ghana. Walking through the campus, I was struck by the youthful energy and lively debates taking place. It was a hub of intellectual activity, where students discussed topics ranging from African politics to global economics, reflecting the country's hopes and challenges. Meeting professors and students gave me insights not just into Ghanaian academia, but also into the aspirations driving the nation's younger generation.

These experiences, shaped by Kojo's steady patience, helped me piece together the diverse layers of Ghanaian life. His introductions and insights served as bridges over cultural divides, helping me understand the many facets of this new environment. With each day, my appreciation for the depth of Accra grew, and every lesson brought me closer to transitioning from being an outsider to becoming an active participant.

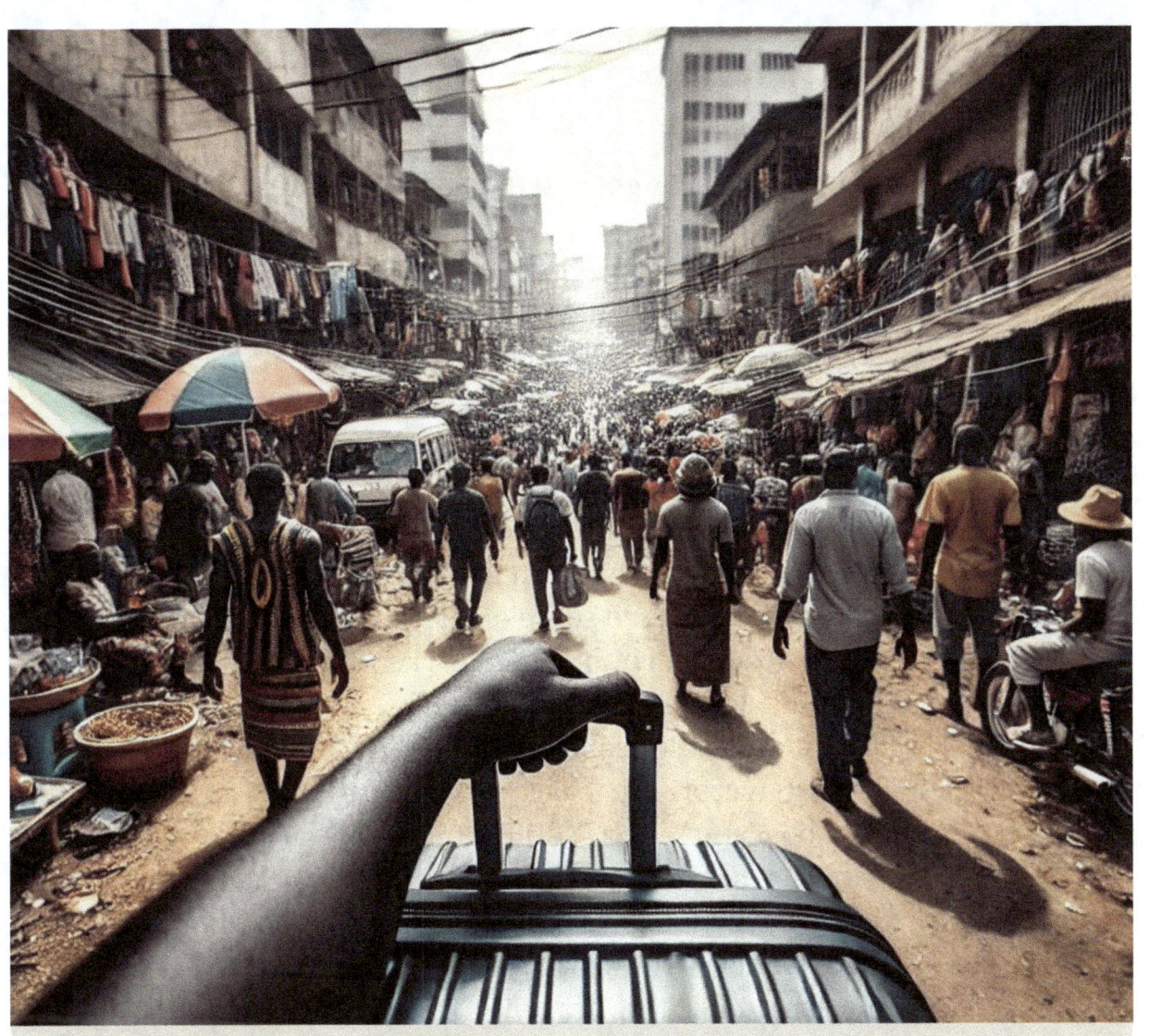

I hadn't arrived in Ghana for more than ten minutes before I found myself kicked out of a cab, standing with acquaintances referred to show me around. As I looked at the chaotic scene unfolding around us, it felt as if I was still very much alone. The streets were alive with sounds of honking cars, screaming pedestrians, and a flurry of movement that seemed to have no clear order. As I took it all in, the reality of my situation hit me hard. This wasn't going to be a typical journey. I realized this mission would test me in unexpected ways, and adaptability would have to be my greatest ally.

The Hunt For An Apartment / Reflections on a Dream Deferred

My search for a permanent home in Accra was both challenging and enlightening. With Kojo's guidance, each apartment viewing revealed the harsh realities of the local housing market, where landlords charged foreigners exorbitant prices. This exposure to local opportunism was a sobering reminder of the complications involved in settling into Africa.

The search also highlighted the tension between identity and economic opportunism, clashing with the idealistic visions of the Year of Return. There was no shared sense of 'blackness' or diasporic solidarity here; instead, I encountered a marketplace eager to exploit my status as an outsider. After numerous difficult negotiations, we finally secured a clean, well-maintained apartment in the heart of Osu. Though somewhat overpriced, it was a welcoming space amidst the city's hustle and bustle—a place I could tentatively call my own.

Settling in deepened my understanding of Accra's social and physical landscape. Open ditches replaced sidewalks, and the buzz of mosquitoes hinted at ever-present health risks. This tempered my initial romanticism with a dose of reality, reshaping my view of what it means to return to a homeland that felt both familiar and foreign.

As I packed my bags to move into the new apartment, I reflected on the whirlwind of my first weeks in Accra. The city had challenged my assumptions and tested my resilience. Accra was not the welcoming homeland I had envisioned; instead, it presented a complex, sometimes harsh reality. Yet, amidst these challenges, the city also revealed the unyielding spirit of its people and the small acts of kindness that made everyday life bearable.

Though I came searching for roots, what I found was a profound lesson in the ramifications of identity and belonging. My journey is far from over, but as I prepare to settle into my new home, I carry with me a mix of hard-earned wisdom and cautious optimism. Perhaps what I'm truly searching for isn't just a physical place to settle, but a deeper sense of peace with my heritage and the realities of my new environment. This evolving understanding drives my determination to navigate and embrace the many layers of life in Accra, marking the beginning of a new chapter in my exploration of identity and home.

City Life in Osu / Street Observations / Load shedding

Establishing myself in Osu, just off the lively Oxford Street in central Accra, was like stepping straight into the vibrant pulse of the city. Initially, the vibrancy was electrifying, with the streets pulsing to rhythms that promised endless new discoveries. However, as the novelty began to fade, the glossy veneer started to peel back, revealing layers of a more complex and often unsettling reality. Many locals, while outwardly friendly, quickly branded me a "Yankee"—an outsider seemingly ripe for exploitation.This label shaped every interaction, from routine transactions where people tried to take advantage, to deeper attempts at forming genuine connections, often clouded by mistrust and hidden agendas.

Amidst this environment, Rasta, the middle-aged housekeeper with a love for reggae and dreadlocks that swept down his back, stood out as a beacon of sincerity. Though he expected a tip for his services, his assistance always came from the heart, offering a rare glimpse of genuine connection in the day-to-day grind.

As I wandered the streets of Osu for hours, I immersed myself in the vivid panorama of daily life, with each outing enriching my grasp of Accra's complex social dynamics. The city buzzed with an infectious hustle, tinged with less savory elements.

One particularly striking observation was the casual nature of public urination—men and women alike unconcerned with privacy or decorum, openly relieving themselves. This blatant lack of public decency reflected the backward nature and norms I was encountering.

Adding to the daily problems was the persistent issue of load shedding, where power could be out for hours at a time. During these blackouts, preparing meals became impossible, and food spoilage was a real concern. The stifling heat made the indoors unbearable at times, driving everyone to the streets. These impromptu gatherings became communal vents where people openly discussed the country's myriad problems. Ironically, while load shedding was a significant hardship, it also served as a catalyst for community bonding. Residents shared their frustrations and hopes, making the best of the challenging conditions by coming together in solidarity. This paradoxical silver lining highlighted a resilient spirit, as the community found ways to cope and connect amidst the adversity.

Despite these challenges, the street vendors infused the city with vibrant energy. Buying fresh coconuts turned into a daily ritual that deeply connected me to the city. Recognizing my frequent visits, my regular vendor began delivering coconuts directly to my apartment. With expert precision, he would slice them open and pour the water into a jug, a gesture that soon became a cherished part of my daily routine.

Culinary Adventures and Challenges

Exploring Ghana's culinary landscape became an adventure of its own, with Kojo eagerly guiding me through the flavors of his culture. Our food excursions often turned into fiery trials, as the staple dishes —like Banku served with spicy fish—proved to be more than just a new taste experience. The intense heat of the food left me struggling not only with unfamiliar flavors but also with stomach issues, turning my culinary adventures into tests of endurance.

This forced me to adjust my eating habits. Living in Osu gave me easy access to Shoprite, a well-known supermarket just down the street from my apartment. I soon found myself shopping there more often, seeking ingredients that were gentler on my stomach while still allowing me to incorporate some local flavors. Cooking my own meals became a way to strike a balance between embracing Ghanaian cuisine and sticking to what my system could handle.

Traversing the local economy added another layer to my adjustment. The Ghanaian cedi, exchanging at around five to the dollar, quickly made it clear that my money wouldn't stretch as far as I had hoped. Expat guides had painted Ghana as a budget-friendly destination, but the reality I encountered told a different story. Budgeting became a critical skill—not just for getting by day to day but for preserving some of the lifestyle I had envisioned. Every purchase required thought, as I balanced the desire to fully engage with local culture against the need to manage my finances carefully. The cost of buying less spicy, more familiar foods only deepened my understanding of Accra's economic terrain.

These experiences—from my culinary misadventures to the unexpected financial hurdles—gave me a deeper understanding of life in Accra. They showed me just how important it was to stay flexible and adapt as I continued to find my way through this lively yet challenging new environment.

The Shadow of White Supremacy

Living in Osu, I saw firsthand the lingering effects of colonialism and economic inequality in Accra. The local economy was dominated by major companies, mostly owned by foreigners—Whites, Arabs, Chinese, and Lebanese. Despite being in a predominantly Black nation, economic control rested with a minority elite, echoing a dynamic all too familiar, one that highlighted the long-standing grip of colonialism and white supremacy.

What struck me even more was the special treatment given to white foreigners. As I walked through the streets, I noticed how they were often treated like gods. Ghanaians would go out of their way to accommodate these visitors, sometimes to extreme lengths, even bowing or kissing the ground in front of them. This differed from the pride and defiance I had seen growing up in Black American communities. Seeing such acts of submission was difficult to accept.

As I tried to make sense of this behavior, it became clear that many locals didn't recognize the deeper issues at play. To them, showing favor to whites seemed natural, perhaps even admirable. They didn't fully grasp how these interactions reinforced unequal power dynamics. Unlike the resistance often found in Black communities in the U.S., there was an acceptance here, which only added to my sense of isolation.

Another troubling aspect was the widespread use of skin-bleaching products. For the first time, I saw products openly sold to people seeking to lighten their skin. This pursuit of fairer skin, shaped by colonial influence and racial preferences, revealed deeper issues related to identity and self-worth. The sight of these products on store shelves served as a harsh reminder of how ideals of whiteness had deeply infiltrated the culture and mindset.

These cultural and historical disconnects were some of the hardest challenges I faced. Every day, I was reminded of the deep divide between my worldview and that of the locals, amplifying the feeling of being an outsider. The scars of colonialism had shaped attitudes and perceptions in profound ways, making it clear how deeply embedded these influences were.This environment, where foreign influences held such sway, combined with the pursuit of whiteness through skin bleaching, showed just how much colonialism had shaped societal values and behaviors.

As a Black American committed to pro-Black ideals and Pan-Africanism, I felt particularly isolated. The lack of a strong Pan-African sentiment in daily life and the visible remnants of colonial influence left me questioning whether I could find common ground in a place where such ideologies seemed to have little relevance.

White God, Black Land

In Ghana, Christian devotion runs even deeper than what I observed among Black communities in the Mississippi Delta. As I wandered through the streets, I was struck by the prominent depictions of a white Jesus, while traditional African spiritual symbols were noticeably absent. Curious, I decided to attend a neighborhood church service. It turned out to be a profoundly energetic and theatrical display of faith.

The ceremony was both captivating and unsettling. The congregation's passionate prayers and hymns seemed to blur the line between faith and performance, creating an atmosphere of intense spiritual fervor.

However, the most striking moment came when I asked a preacher why there were no Black or African deities in the church's imagery. His response was swift and harsh: I was chased off with a belt, a reaction as violent as it was revealing.

This shocking encounter exposed a troubling reality that extends far beyond Ghana, affecting both Africans and Black Americans—the lingering effects of mental colonization. Even in a predominantly Black nation, the rejection of divine figures that reflect African culture revealed just how deeply colonial indoctrination runs. It became clear that mental liberation is essential to achieving true spiritual and cultural freedom.

Load shedding was one of the biggest adjustments I had to make after leaving the U.S. for Africa. The lights could cut out at any moment, plunging entire neighborhoods into darkness—no warning, no pattern. Each blackout left me feeling exposed, at the mercy of forces I couldn't control. The streets held a scene my writing could hardly capture—a mix of chaos, fear, and quiet anticipation. Crowds would gather, everyone sharing that same uneasy jolt, whispering about conspiracies, wondering if this was more than just power shortages. In those moments, the tension hung heavy in the air, like we were all bracing for something worse.

While exploring Accra, the presence of white supremacy was impossible to overlook. Most major businesses were still controlled by whites, Asians, or Arabs, with African men often serving as the public face. It was a dynamic that felt both unsettlingly familiar and out of place at the same time. What struck me even more, though, was how deeply this influence had infiltrated religion. Christianity here had a particularly intense grip—almost like a possession, with people clinging to it so fervently that it felt unsettling. It was as if the religion had taken hold of their very spirits, reflecting a legacy of control that ran far deeper than I had imagined.

Night Out in Accra with Kojo

Kojo was eager to introduce me to the vibrant nightlife of Accra, so one evening, he took me to a well-known club renowned for its high energy and pulsating music. As Afrobeats and dancehall rhythms filled the air, the dance floor buzzed with infectious enthusiasm. As we settled into the scene, Kojo pointed out a more sobering aspect of the nightlife. "Look closely," he said. "Many of these glamorous women are involved in prostitution. It's part of the commerce here." His words cast a new light on the surroundings, revealing a layer of the club's atmosphere that was as much about business as it was about entertainment.

That night, I made a meaningful connection with a beautiful woman who managed the front of the club. She was from the Edo tribe in Nigeria, and her warm demeanor stood out against the club's chaotic energy. We struck up a conversation, and she shared her experiences of life in Ghana, offering insights into both the challenges and opportunities she encountered. Her stories deepened my understanding of Accra, revealing the dimensions hidden beneath the surface of its vibrant nightlife.

Our friendship quickly became important, offering not just companionship but also a window into the intricate dynamics of Accra's lively yet complicated social scene. However, my interactions with others often revealed a more transactional side of relationships. Many of the women I met seemed to see me as an opportunity for personal gain, viewing me as a "come up" rather than a potential friend. Even when conversations felt friendly, there was often a hidden agenda beneath the surface—a calculated effort to position themselves, rather than seeking a genuine connection.

I also crossed paths with Ghanaian American women who were there visiting from the U.S., but even those interactions felt strained. Many seemed uninterested in building connections, influenced by the lingering racial hatred toward Black Americans that they brought with them. This added another layer of nuance, making it harder to navigate authentic relationships in a social environment where personal motives often overshadowed genuine bonds. These experiences shed light on the challenges within Accra's social scene, reflecting the broader difficulties of identity and connection within the diaspora.

Sundays at Labadi Beach

Sundays in Accra offered the perfect escape to Labadi Beach, the city's most lively coastal hotspot. While the rest of the city slowed down, Labadi buzzed with an energy that rivaled San Diego's famous beaches, like Pacific and Mission. The air pulsed with the sounds of reggae, hip-hop, and afrobeat, attracting a diverse crowd and creating a dynamic scene that showcased the essence of Ghana—its vibrant culture and breathtaking natural beauty.

The atmosphere at Labadi was one of pure joy and connection, as families, friends, and visitors—including Black Americans, Nigerians, and locals—gathered beneath colorful sun umbrellas. The ocean breeze blended the sounds of laughter with the sizzle of nearby grills, creating a scene that felt both celebratory and close-knit. The beach buzzed with life, offering a vivid snapshot of the warmth and hospitality that define the Ghanaian spirit.

However, despite its vibrant atmosphere, Labadi Beach faced significant environmental challenges. The waters, often clouded with floating debris like discarded clothing, detracted from its natural appeal. The shoreline, scattered with trash, revealed the effects of poor waste management. This neglect highlighted a broader issue in Ghana's urban areas, where the community's vitality was often hindered by inadequate infrastructure.

Yet each visit to Labadi reminded me of what made Accra special —not just as a city, but as a cultural hub. The mix of the beach's lively energy and its environmental challenges revealed a deeper story of a nation grappling with rapid urbanization, often without the infrastructure to keep up. Sundays at Labadi were more than just a break from the daily grind; they were a celebration of fun and freedom, offering one of the most enjoyable beach experiences I've ever had, despite the imperfections. The spirit of the people and the communal joy outshined the physical flaws, reflecting a resilient community that thrives even in the face of adversity.

Confronting History at Osu Castle

Visiting Osu Castle, a place I had longed to see, became one of the most unsettling experiences of my time in Ghana. I had expected to feel a deep connection to this painful part of history, imagining a visceral bond with the suffering and resilience of my ancestors. But the reality was far from what I had imagined. As I approached the entrance, I saw a white visitor ahead of me welcomed with smiles and warmth. When it was my turn, everything changed. The warmth vanished, replaced by cold suspicion. I was accused of trespassing and dismissed without a shred of respect. Forced to leave, I was left grappling with the bitter irony.

Standing on the beach beside the Gulf of Guinea, the waves seemed to whisper hard truths. It's said my ancestors were torn from this very soil, bound for horrors across the Atlantic. But as I stood there, the ancestral connection I longed for never materialized. Instead, I felt a hollow emptiness. "'I'm not from here,' I whispered into the wind, my voice carrying both defiance and sorrow."

My grandmother's words echoed in my mind—her unwavering claim that we were not Africans, but from a native tribe in Arkansas. This disconnect between my expectations and the reality of the moment shook me to my core.

As the ocean breeze carried my words into the vast, indifferent sea, a wave of sadness and anger welled up inside me. Osu Castle, a haunting symbol of past atrocities, seemed to turn its back on me, offering no acknowledgment of our shared history. The rejection was a bitter pill, deepening my sense of isolation and alienation. In this land where I had hoped to find belonging, I was instead faced with a painful reminder of my otherness.

This experience at Osu Castle not only revealed the lingering shadows of colonial attitudes but also highlighted the complex dynamics of identity and belonging for those in the diaspora seeking to reconnect with their roots. Though shaken, my resolve to forge a connection with Africa remained intact. Yet the pain of that day left a lasting mark on my soul—a reminder of the long journey ahead in bridging the vast gap between the Africa of my imagination and the reality of its present.

A Test of Determination / The Journey to a Ghanaian Driver's License

Despite the many challenges I faced, my determination to embrace life in Ghana remained unwavering. My journey to assimilation took a practical turn when I decided to obtain a Ghanaian driver's license—a process that soon became one of my most trying experiences.

I reconnected with Ama, who had welcomed me upon my arrival, hoping her guidance would simplify the process. However, what started as a straightforward task quickly became a gauntlet of exploitation and bureaucratic obstacles. Everyone I encountered seemed to view me not as someone seeking a fresh start, but as an opportunity for personal gain. The spirit of the "Year of Return" felt distant and hollow as I navigated a system steeped in greed and opportunism.

The licensing office was no different. I was quoted a shocking 3,000 cedis—far more than fair or expected. Reluctantly, I paid the fee, eager to move forward, but it left me feeling exploited. After handing over the money, I was told to wait two weeks for the license to be processed. During this waiting period, anxiety set in, and I couldn't shake the doubt that I had been swindled.

As I waded through this bureaucratic maze, a subtle weakness began to creep through my body—a faint but persistent feeling that something was off. It was a quiet, nagging whisper, reminding me that not all challenges are visible, and some threats come unseen.

Finally, after weeks of uncertainty, my Ghanaian driver's license arrived—a bittersweet victory. While I was relieved to have it in hand, the process had taken its toll on my relationships with Ama and Kojo. The delays fueled my suspicions of being scammed, leading to tense exchanges and accusations. Their reactions to my concerns deepened the rift between us, casting a shadow over friendships once rooted in trust and camaraderie.

Though I had successfully navigated the bureaucratic corruption, it came at the cost of personal connections. Amidst these struggles, the weakness in my body had grown stronger, hinting at a deeper illness. What began as a faint sign was now intensifying, hinting at an even greater, silent challenge to my health.

Trials and Transition

After a month and a half of exploring Accra, my curiosity to see more of Ghana grew. Hetty recommended Mompong in the Eastern Region, a place that sparked my imagination with the promise of new landscapes and experiences.

As I made plans to relocate, the ailment returned with renewed intensity. What had begun as mild discomfort quickly escalated into severe diarrhea, leaving me weak and barely able to stand. The timing couldn't have been worse, and the idea of moving felt daunting.

During this turmoil, the friendship I had formed with my Edo friend became a lifeline. When the illness overwhelmed me, she stepped in, providing care beyond what I could have expected. She cooked, brought medicine, and stayed by my side, helping me through the worst of it. Despite her efforts, my condition rapidly worsened. I lost 30 pounds in just four days, a staggering physical toll, leaving me almost unrecognizable.

Still determined to follow through with my plans, Hetty connected me with her friend Bonsu, a real estate expert familiar with properties outside central Accra. Together, we ventured out to explore potential living spaces, navigating the bustling Madina Market just north of Osu. The market was crowded, with vendors lining the dirt roads. It wasn't ideal, and with night falling, reaching Mompong became impractical. Sick and exhausted, I reluctantly settled for a flat in Madina.

The flat was dreadful—a small room along a muddy, barely passable road, costing 50 cedis per day. The conditions were dire, with ant piles and pests everywhere, but my need for rest outweighed any desire for comfort. Bonsu assured me this was only temporary, a brief stop until we could find something better. Even Hetty, upon visiting, was shocked by the state of the room, noting that it was worse than anything she had seen—even by local standards.

As the night wore on, my health took a turn for the worse. By morning, I could no longer bear the sickness. In desperation, I noticed a clinic next door—a place I hadn't seen before. The staff acted quickly, running blood tests that confirmed what I had only heard of in stories: MALARIA. Immediate treatment was essential.

The speed and efficiency of the clinic staff in diagnosing and treating me took me by surprise, especially considering the slow, frustrating healthcare processes I was used to in the U.S. I had barely settled in before they had taken blood samples, confirmed the malaria diagnosis, and administered a shot along with some pills. The relief was almost immediate—a testament to the effectiveness and accessibility of healthcare here, despite the many challenges the country faces.

In those moments, it was hard not to reflect on the efficiency of Ghana's emergency care, which felt far more responsive than the bureaucratic delays and red tape I was used to back home. The country may struggle with infrastructure, but when it comes to saving lives, Ghana acts quickly. As I reflected on my ordeal, the region's historical nickname, "the white man's graveyard," came to mind. The phrase now struck with a chilling clarity. In some ways, the reputation had lived up to its ominous origin.

That day at the Gulf of Guinea, after the betrayal at the slave castle, was heavy. As I stood there, staring out at the endless ocean, I expected to feel some deep connection. Yet nothing came. Instead, a cold whisper seemed to creep through my veins, carried by the wind off the water. My grandma's voice reached out to comfort me from the sky, reminding me we weren't African but from a native Black tribe in Arkansas. It all hit at once—the weight of what I had seen and the emptiness in my chest. My spirit stirred restlessly, and before I knew it, the words came out of my mouth like a revelation: I'm not from here.

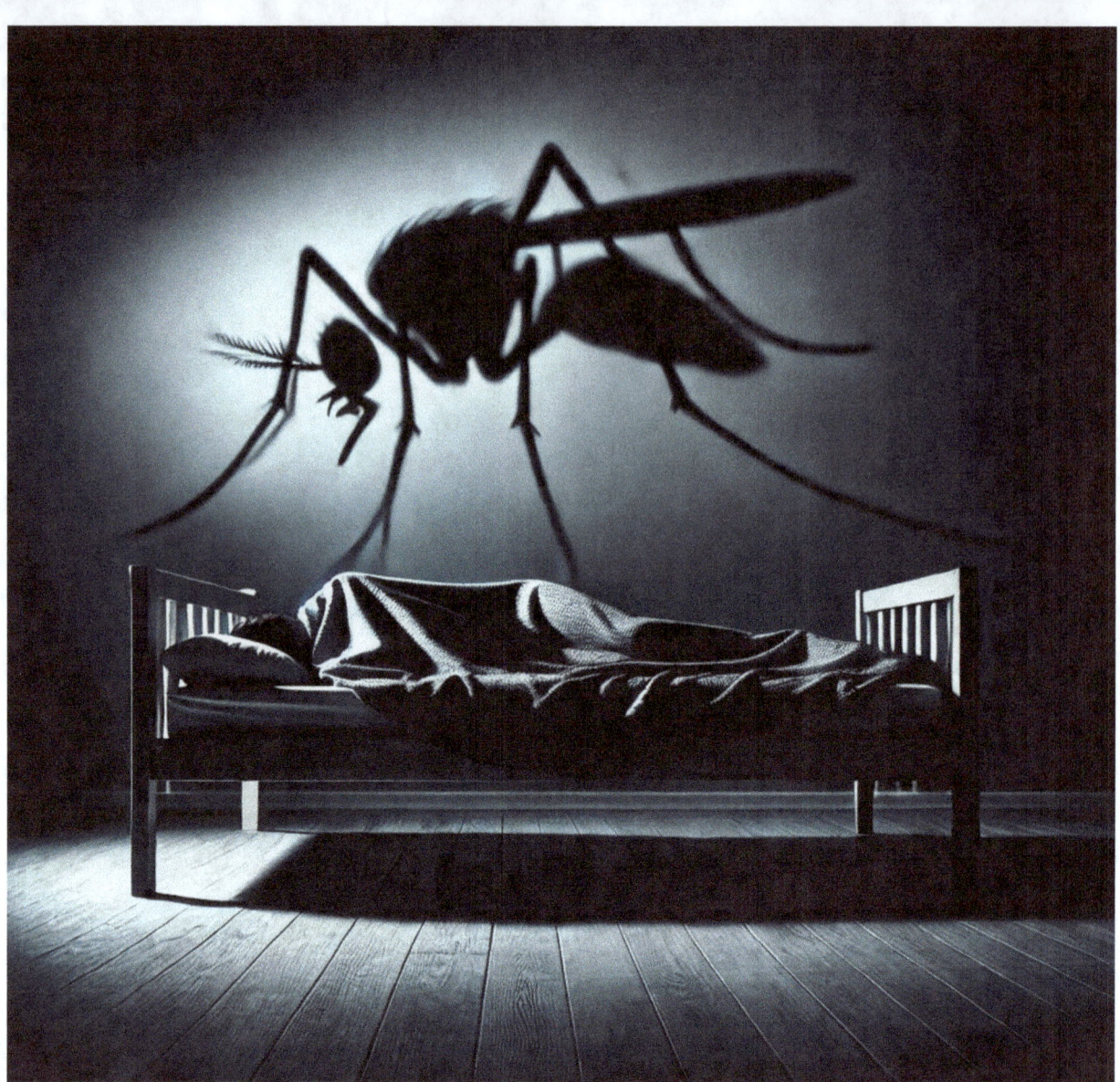

The deadly mosquito preyed on me every night, leaving me curled beneath the covers, its relentless buzzing a reminder that they ruled this space. No matter how hard I tried to protect myself, they always found a way through. Out here, it wasn't lions or wild beasts that struck fear in me—it was the invisible threat of malaria. Though curable, anyone unfamiliar with the signs or unaware of their illness could easily lose their life. Each buzz in the dark felt like a warning, reminding me that the real danger was unseen but always close.

A New Chapter in Mompong

The next day, I took some time to explore Madina's vibrant market—a bustling hub where anything you could imagine seemed within reach. The market was alive with color and sound, vendors calling out from stalls overflowing with fresh produce, handmade crafts, and fabrics of every hue. The smell of grilled meats mingled with the scent of spices in the air, making it impossible not to get caught up in the energy of the place. As I soaked in the lively atmosphere, Bonsu arrived with good news: he had secured a place for me in Mompong, and I was more than ready to leave behind the cramped, uncomfortable conditions of my current room.

Together, we boarded one of Ghana's tro-tros, the local buses that were often packed with people but always full of character, and set off for the Eastern Region. The journey felt like an adventure, with the bus winding up steep hills that revealed stunning views of the lush, green landscape. The farther we got from Accra, the more the scenery seemed to open up—rolling hills dotted with small villages, palm trees swaying in the breeze. When we finally reached the top, it felt as if we'd stepped into another world—a quiet, village-like setting, far removed from the hustle and chaos of Accra.

The place Bonsu had found for me was tucked away down a dirt road, surrounded by bush. Yet, it was the nicest accommodation I had seen so far. The small house had clean, simple furnishings, with windows that opened out to the vast greenery surrounding it. Although slightly overpriced, the tranquility and quality of the room made it worth every cedi. In this peaceful setting, I finally felt a sense of relief, a reprieve from the noise and commotion that had defined my stay in Accra. For the first time in a while, I could breathe freely, appreciating the quiet beauty of my new surroundings.

While at the apartment, I met other Black Americans, including an older man in his late 60s, his wife, and their son, who was in his mid-20s. The older man was approachable, and we quickly bonded over our shared reasons for leaving America—a search for peace and respite from the racism that had tainted our experiences back home.

Our conversation was refreshing, but it soon took a somber turn when he shared his own story of exploitation. He had fallen victim to a devastating scam, purchasing fake land in a deal that cost him dearly. It was a loss he was still struggling to recover from. His story was disheartening and highlighted the harsh reality of exploitation, even for those seeking a new beginning in their ancestral homeland. It reinforced my own concerns about local dealings and the need to stay vigilant. The painful truth was that the dream of returning to one's roots could be easily tainted by those looking to take advantage of the hopeful and trusting.

As I adjusted to my new home in Mompong, I reflected on these stories and my own experiences. They revealed a complex mix of hope, disillusionment, and the ongoing search for a place where one can truly belong. My encounter with the older gentleman wasn't just a sharing of similar tales; it was a reminder of the challenges that come with trying to reclaim a heritage in a land that felt both distant and indifferent. If they could deceive an elder Black American man, it was clear they wouldn't hesitate to do the same to someone younger like myself.

Village Life

In my new area, I found myself adapting to the distinct rhythms of village life. Unlike the bustling urban environment of Accra, life here was less convenient but more connected to the land. The pace was slower, and the relationship with nature more direct, with many locals growing their own food and relying on natural resources for their daily needs.

I visited Bonsu at his place of business to catch up and learn more about the village lifestyle. He ran a local barbershop, which also doubled as a printing service for residents—an essential amenity in an area where such services were hard to come by. What surprised me even more was that Bonsu spent his evenings teaching, a reflection of his deep commitment to the community and his versatile intellect. His profound understanding of both the local culture and the broader educational landscape made him an invaluable guide as I transitioned from city to village life.

Educational Insights and Cultural Norms

As I spent more time in Mompong, I began attending Bonsu's evening math classes. His teaching was impressive, surpassing that of university professors I had encountered in the States. During these sessions, I noticed that all the young women had very short hair. Curious, I asked Bonsu about it. He explained that in the community, long hair was seen as a distraction and believed to make the girls appear less intelligent. Most girls, except those in private schools, were required to keep their hair short to encourage focus and discipline.

Curious about how the students felt about the rule, I spoke with several of the young women. They shared their frustration, explaining that having their hair cut short diminished their sense of individuality and femininity, affecting their self-esteem. What was meant to promote discipline clearly had a deeper personal impact than I had realized.

As I spent more time with Bonsu and met more people, I was touched by how welcoming everyone was. It was a close-knit community where neighbors knew and supported each other. Despite certain rigid expectations, the warmth and unity revealed the strong cultural bonds that shaped everyday life, offering a real sense of belonging.

With each day, I learned more about the traditions, values, and practices that defined this place. My immersion into village culture was not just about adjusting to a new way of living, but about gaining a deeper understanding of a world so far from mine.

A Glimpse into Village Prosperity

Our visit to Hetty's home provided a glimpse into her family's daily life and an eye-opening lesson in how wealth is perceived. Her residence, with its large yard and acres of well-tended land, sharply contrasted with the common stereotypes of poverty in African villages. Despite this abundance, many locals still believed they were poor—not because of a lack of resources, but due to comparisons with Western standards of wealth.

Each household in the village had significant resources that would be considered a luxury in much of the world. Hetty's family, like many others, owned their home outright and enjoyed acres of land, free from ongoing property taxes or rent. They grew their own food, maintained personal water wells, and lived without the constant financial pressures that burden so many in the West. In terms of sustainability and self-sufficiency, they had more than 90% of American households. Yet, the locals didn't see it that way.

Many villagers believed they were lacking because they didn't have flashy cars, expensive gadgets, or the consumer-driven lifestyle of the West. Despite having food security, independence, and a deep connection to the land, they saw their traditional way of life as inferior. Their sense of poverty was shaped not by their actual living conditions but by comparisons to external standards of wealth— standards that overlooked the true value of their resources. The real poverty was mental, rooted in the belief that wealth meant material excess rather than sustainable, debt-free living.

This experience made me rethink the meaning of wealth. In Hetty's village, wealth wasn't measured by bank balances but by living off the land, owning property, and being part of a close-knit community. Yet, many villagers overlooked these advantages, feeling their lives were lacking because they didn't match Western ideals of success.

Reflecting on this visit, I saw how deeply this narrative of poverty had taken root, shaped by external influences. What the villagers had was far more valuable than they realized—a level of self-sufficiency and freedom that many in developed countries would envy. It reminded me that true wealth isn't about having more, but recognizing the worth of what you already have.

Exploring Eastern Region

After being in Mompong for over a month, I established a comfortable daily routine that grounded me in the local culture and landscape. Each morning, I would either stroll over to Bonsu's house or meet him at his shop, where he and his worker spent their days. These moments of relaxation became a cherished part of my daily life.

My favorite local dish quickly became "red red," a delicious stew made with black-eyed peas, red palm oil, plantain, gari, onions, and tomatoes. The sweet, rich flavor made it not only a comforting meal but also a staple of my daily diet. It was filling and energizing, something I looked forward to each day.

One memorable day, Bonsu, Hetty, and I ventured out to explore more of the Eastern Region. We visited several notable sites, including the Aburi Botanical Gardens—an expansive area of over 60 hectares, where trees had been planted by colonial administrators in the late 1800s. The historical and natural beauty of the gardens was breathtaking, offering a serene escape and a vivid reminder of Ghana's colonial past intertwined with its natural heritage.

Our journey continued through the villages of Mamfe, Akropong, Adukrom, and Koforidua, culminating in a visit to Boti Falls, a stunning waterfall. The trip to the falls was both exhilarating and challenging. Our guide, a member of the Ghanaian army, expertly navigated the steep, mountainous terrain with impressive speed and agility. My choice of sandals and the cumbersome camera I carried made the climb difficult, but reaching the waterfall felt like discovering a hidden treasure. The view of the cascading water against the lush greenery was magical, creating a moment of profound beauty and peace that I will cherish forever.

This exploration of Ghana's Eastern Region not only deepened my appreciation for the country's diverse landscapes and rich history but also strengthened my bond with Hetty and Bonsu. Each day in Mompong enriched my understanding of Ghana, leaving me with lasting memories of the food, friendships, and adventures that made my time there unforgettable.

Village Bonds

As time passed, my circle of friends expanded, most notably with the introduction to Barbara, a talented local chef, and her family. Bonsu, ever the connector, brought us together, and I was immediately drawn to Barbara's warmth and incredible culinary skills. She was not only beautiful but also a culinary master, and I soon found myself spending most of my days in the comforting presence of her family.

Barbara's family ran a small shop with their home right behind it, a setup common among local vendors. Their hospitality was heartwarming; they welcomed me as one of their own, sharing meals, laughter, and stories. Barbara's cooking quickly became a highlight of my days, especially her pastries, which were easily the best I'd ever tasted. But it was her jollof rice that won me over completely. Having heard of the infamous 'Jollof wars' back in the United States—where Ghanaians, Nigerians, and Senegalese all claimed superiority—I was now in a position to cast my vote. After trying all versions with an unbiased palate, I could confidently say that Ghana's jollof was the best.

Our days were rich with cultural exchanges, deepening my understanding of Ghanaian life. A few weeks into our friendship, Barbara's twin sisters, both teachers, arrived. They taught me words in Akan, helping me navigate the local markets and ensuring I got fair prices—a great relief, given how my accent often marked me as an outsider.

The companionship of Barbara and her sisters gave me a fresh perspective on relationships; their caring and harmonious nature was unlike the interactions I had often seen back home. Their kindness, combined with the warmth of the community, made my time in Mompong more than just a stay—it was a deeply enriching experience. The ease with which they embraced me helped soften the occasional pangs of homesickness.

Surrounded by new friends who felt like family, I found a sense of home that went beyond geography. It taught me that warmth and kinship could be discovered in the most unexpected places.

It was surprising to see the wealth Hetty and other families in the village possessed, yet many believed they had nothing. This made me realize just how powerful the media was in shaping people's perceptions. Despite Ghana's abundant resources, many were eager to give it all up for a chance to live in America. Some even begged for money, unaware that they often had more than I did. The media convinced them that what they had wasn't enough, despite sitting on untapped potential.

The Struggle for Land in Ghana

As my time in Ghana shifted from exploratory adventures to more purpose-driven missions, the task of securing land revealed a reality far different from the hopeful promises of the Year of Return. What I initially imagined to be a straightforward process, much like property dealings in the United States, turned into an ordeal steeped in deceit and exploitation.

Buoyed by visions of building a life on ancestral soil, my enthusiasm was soon dampened by the difficulties of the Ghanaian real estate market. Unlike the regulated processes back in America, transactions were ambiguous. Potential landowners were often forced to deal directly with individuals claiming knowledge of available plots, a system ripe for abuse. As Bonsu explained, it was common for so-called realtors to showcase beautiful land, claim it was for sale, and then vanish after receiving payment, leaving the buyer to face disputes with the real landowners.

This pattern of fraud wasn't just a cautionary tale—it mirrored the experience of the older Black man from my apartment complex, who had been duped by fake land deals. Despite months of diligent searching, every lead I pursued dissolved into more examples of the dishonesty that plagued the system. Even Bonsu, with all his local connections and insight, found himself unable to navigate the corruption that seemed too deeply entrenched to overcome.

As these revelations surfaced, so did my disillusionment with the personal connections I had formed. It became evident that many of the relationships were transactional, based more on assumptions about my wealth as an American than on genuine friendship. The unraveling of these bonds was painful.

Hetty, someone I had considered a close friend, revealed her true intentions when she began pressuring me to fund her school and provide resources. When I explained that I couldn't meet her demands, the warmth of our friendship quickly faded, marking a sharp change in her attitude.

This cascade of disappointments led to a sobering realization: the Ghana I encountered was far removed from the idyllic return to roots often celebrated in diaspora narratives. Corruption, idolization of whiteness, decaying infrastructure, and a fragmented sense of Black identity created a complex and contradictory reality. As I struggled with these challenges, my dream of establishing roots here began to unravel. The betrayal, the dishonesty, and superficial relationships painted a picture far different from what I had envisioned.

Reflecting on these trials, I began to question whether Ghana, with all its unresolved issues, could truly offer the sanctuary I had been seeking. What was meant to be a journey of reconnection instead became a lesson in the deep differences between the dreams of the diaspora and the realities of life on the ground. Far from finding a welcoming new home, I found a country still grappling with its own identity and integrity. It left me wondering if this land could ever be the haven I had hoped for, or if I was chasing a dream that wasn't yet ready to take root here.

I wasn't accustomed to the backstabbing nature I encountered in Ghana. There was virtually no one to trust, and trying to obtain honest land was impossible in this web of deceit. The "Year of Return" wasn't about reconnecting with heritage—it was a money grab, exploiting the struggles of Black Americans searching for freedom. I expected this kind of exploitation from the white man, but seeing the African people not only aware of it but complicit in the game shook me to my core. It was a betrayal I never expected.

As I searched for land and camaraderie, I felt a growing isolation. The Pan-African ideal I had chased seemed to slip further away the harder I reached for it, like a shadow fading in the distance. The truth was undeniable: Black solidarity, as I had imagined it, didn't exist here. For those in the diaspora hoping to find it, don't waste your time. The reality is harsher than the dream. From children to elders, everyone saw me as an outsider to exploit. The hope I carried was crushed under the weight of deception. What I thought was a shared vision of unity was merely a mirage, vanishing as I approached.

Parting Reflections, Disillusionment and Departure

As the harsh realities of Ghana weighed on me, I found solace in my apartment, researching other African destinations. Intriguingly, my attention was captured by a video of the rap group Migos performing in Johannesburg. The modern vibe and the adoption of Black American culture by the locals resonated with me. Curious, I delved deeper into Johannesburg's lifestyle through YouTube, fascinated by its apparent modernity compared to what I had experienced in Ghana.

Concerns about Johannesburg's high crime rate loomed, yet the need to leave Ghana was paramount. With a heavy heart but firm resolve, I packed my belongings, bidding farewell to Bonsu and Barbara, along with her family. Before my departure, I managed to secure a room online in Johannesburg, hoping it would be a smoother transition than my arrival in Ghana.

I reached out to Kojo, hoping to stay with him one last night before my departure. Despite our previous fallout, he agreed, though the atmosphere was strained—Kojo remained distant, cloistered in his room, leaving me alone with my thoughts. That evening, while stepping out on Oxford Street to pick up some essentials, I had an encounter that symbolized much of my experience in Ghana. Dressed sharply, I was abruptly confronted by a white woman who, with an air of religious zeal, told me I was "nothing without God." When she heard my accent, she recoiled and quickly retreated. This brief interaction spoke volumes, a reminder of the lingering missionary mindset still present in Ghana, intent on reinforcing a sense of inferiority among the locals. It was a poignant moment that encapsulated the societal fractures I had encountered throughout my time here.

My final hours in Ghana were as tumultuous as my stay. At the airport, an attempt to extort money from me under the pretext of overstaying my visa encapsulated the relentless exploitation I had faced. This wasn't the 'Year of Return' I had imagined—it was more like the 'Year of Deception and Backstabbing.' Though I resisted and was eventually let go, the ordeal left a bitter taste.

As I boarded my flight, there was no sorrow in leaving, only relief. I had come seeking a home—a place I believed would welcome me with open arms, a land I thought was mine by heritage. But as I reflected on my time here, I realized this journey had been less about rediscovering my roots and more about surviving a gauntlet of exploitation. Ghana, for all its beauty and warmth, was also steeped in a culture of opportunism that left me feeling betrayed.

This was a brutal lesson in the reality of reconnecting with an ancestral home. It's a warning for Black Americans chasing romanticized visions of the motherland. The idea of 'home' is powerful, but the truth is often far uglier than the fantasy sold to us. What I thought was a return to where my ancestors came from became a harsh realization: spiritually, and in every remnant of their memory, I knew my ancestors were never from here.

Ghana Recap

Ghana's welcoming spirit drew me in. I delighted in the local cuisine, soaked in the serene landscapes, and appreciated the rich cultural heritage. Yet, my journey was overshadowed by challenges. The search for land, which I had hoped would be straightforward, quickly turned into a maze of corruption and deception. What should have been a smooth process became riddled with mistrust, tarnishing the experience.

These experiences revealed the problems within Ghana—a land rich in history and potential, yet mired in opportunism and exploitation. The narrative of the 'Year of Return' often hid the difficult realities on the ground. More disheartening was realizing the Ghanaian government's lack of real commitment to development. What was presented as an invitation home felt more like a calculated move to exploit Black Americans' yearning for roots. It was crafted to profit from the pain of the Black diaspora without offering genuine connection or empathy.

The legacy of the transatlantic slave trade still runs deep in this region, not only in memory but in the way people interact. The betrayal and deceit I faced echoed that tragic history—where Africans were once sold, I could still feel the remnants of exploitation today in the backstabbing and manipulation. This behavior felt like a product of centuries of betrayal and commodification.

As I reflect, I realize I never truly felt at home here. There was no spiritual connection, no sense of belonging—something I had been too eager to overlook in my pursuit of Pan-African unity. Out of respect for Africa, I tolerated things I wouldn't elsewhere. The mistreatment I faced, which I would have easily challenged in other places, became harder to ignore. It became clear that this was not my home; my spirit didn't resonate with this land, and it reaffirmed that my ancestors were not from here.

As I prepare to move on to South Africa, I do so with invaluable lessons. My expectations are tempered, and my resilience is sharpened. This next chapter is more than just a new location—it's a deeper shift in my understanding of home and heritage. I move forward with clearer eyes, ready to face whatever lies ahead with a stronger grasp on reality.

Side Note Intel: The Watchers Among Us

During my months in Ghana, I crossed paths with many Black people from the diaspora, most of whom carried the same dreams of reconnection and rediscovery. But as time passed, I began to notice something unsettling beneath the surface. A significant number of these individuals were not just ordinary travelers or seekers of ancestral roots—they seemed to have other, more covert purposes.

Many were Caribbean Blacks from the States, alongside Black Americans, and their presence often appeared tied to missions less about cultural exploration and more about surveillance. Some operated under the guise of missionaries, while others had connections to shadowy organizations. It became clear that Ghana, with its pull on the diaspora through the 'Year of Return,' also served as a focal point for insidious agendas.

The exploitation I uncovered in my dealings wasn't limited to the locals; it extended to people I might have considered allies. These individuals, who should have been part of the shared journey of seeking and healing, were instead there to observe, report, and gather intel. Their roles, cloaked in spirituality or humanitarian work, often masked strategic missions serving interests far removed from unity and cultural reclamation.

I experienced this firsthand during a strange encounter. One afternoon, while walking home through a wooded area, a Black Caribbean man approached me, his expression stern and his tone cold. Without any pleasantries, he started interrogating me. "What are you really doing in Ghana?" he asked, his voice thick with suspicion. It felt less like curiosity and more like interrogation, as if I had something to hide. In that moment, I realized I was being watched more than I thought, even by other Blacks from the diaspora.

For anyone planning to follow the same path, this serves as a warning: approach with caution and skepticism when dealing with fellow diaspora in Ghana. Every smiling face and shared heritage may not be what it seems. While the land is rich with history and potential, it's also filled with hidden watchers—those ensuring certain narratives are maintained. The exploitation I encountered wasn't just from locals; even supposed allies had hidden motives. Similar to Washington D.C., Ghana is a Black spy capital, where Black operatives move in the shadows, blending effortlessly.

JOHANNESBURG, SOUTH AFRICA
Arrival in Johannesburg / A New Chapter Begins

After a long but exhilarating seven-hour flight from Ghana, I arrived at O.R. Tambo International Airport in Johannesburg. The sleek, modern design immediately caught my attention, reminding me more of top-tier U.S. airports than anything I had seen in West Africa. The atmosphere felt welcoming and professional, unlike the experiences I had in Ghana, and the efficient and helpful airport staff reinforced the feeling that I was stepping into a new chapter.

As I exited the airport, I was greeted by hotel staff holding a sign with my name, offering an organized and reassuring welcome. The drive to my hotel filled me with excitement as I chatted with the driver who introduced me to Johannesburg's local nicknames—"Joburg" or "Jozi." The sleek, modern freeway, bustling with cars and surrounded by signs of industrial growth, gave the impression of a vibrant, forward-moving city, a world apart from what I had left behind. Situated in Gauteng, South Africa's most populated province, Johannesburg felt alive with energy and diversity.

When I arrived at my hotel, I was thrilled to find it nestled in a lively, artsy neighborhood, where people confidently strolled the streets at night and music filled the air—Chris Brown's tracks adding to the urban vibe. My first taste of Joburg's culture was electrifying; the city felt alive, and its energy resonated with me instantly. After checking in and freshening up, I ventured out to explore, mindful of the advice to walk in the streets rather than the sidewalks due to concerns about crime. Though the caution left me slightly on edge, the thrill of discovering a new city outweighed my nerves. Directed to a local hotspot called "Shakers," I found myself impressed by the effortless style and swagger of the South Africans, whose fashion and confidence mirrored the spirit of Black American communities back home.

The night carried on at a rooftop bar, where I met a group of Angolans whose friendliness and engaging conversation added to my growing sense that Johannesburg might be the change I needed. After exchanging contacts with one of the Angolan women, I returned to my hotel, feeling optimistic. The comfort of my modern room was a welcome relief, and as I lay there, I realized that for the first time in a long while, I felt at ease. Maybe Johannesburg was the home I had been searching for all along. The city's energy matched my own, and as I drifted off to sleep, I couldn't help but think, "Now, this feels like home."

Daylight Discoveries in Maboneng

My first morning in Johannesburg began with a burst of curiosity and enthusiasm. Eager to experience the city in daylight, I stepped out from my hotel in Maboneng, a neighborhood renowned for its vibrant, artsy vibe and creative pulse.

I soon met some of my neighbors in the building, and everyone was warm and genuinely welcoming. As I wandered the neighborhood, exploring local stores, I soaked in the vibrant energy of the place. The shop workers were incredibly friendly, reinforcing my positive first impression of the city. One young lady in particular, Lebo from Soweto, was especially helpful in assisting me with getting a SIM card for my phone—a crucial step for staying connected. Meeting someone from the legendary Soweto added authenticity to my urban adventure.

As I strolled through the area, I was captivated by the African art adorning the walls. Unlike in America, where billboards often feature predominantly white figures, here the art celebrated Black pride, filling the streets with creativity and self-expression. The local fashion also stood out—a unique blend of '90s R&B and hip-hop styles fused with Jozi's distinct flair, creating an eclectic and visually engaging street scene.

Fox Street, lined with fine dining options, added a cosmopolitan feel to the neighborhood. To further acclimate myself and gauge its safety, I took a long walk, mapping out the area. Though the heart of the neighborhood felt lively and secure, the outskirts told a different story, reminiscent of some of the roughest neighborhoods in the US. Locals advised caution, especially with jewelry or visible electronics, as they could easily attract unwanted attention. After a tense experience of being followed while wearing a gold chain, I quickly learned to dress modestly and keep valuables hidden.

This blend of artistic allure and gritty reality defines the neighborhood—a place that encapsulates the complexities of Johannesburg. My explorations not only introduced me to its physical spaces but also to the nuanced dynamics of navigating a city that is both inspiring and challenging.

Culinary Delights and Urban Exploration

Within the confines of my apartment building, I discovered a hidden gem—a restaurant that quickly became my go-to spot for incredible meals. The kitchen was helmed by Prisca, a skilled chef from Zambia, while the restaurant itself was owned by Ali, a charismatic entrepreneur from Guinea. This convenient dining option introduced me to South Africa's staple dish, Pap, though similar to Ghana's Banku, was served here with a rich beef stew that instantly became a favorite. When not indulging in Pap, I often opted for the simple pleasure of wings and fries.

As I settled into my surroundings, my curiosity about the city grew. Fortuitously, Ali and I struck up a friendship, bonded by his vision of a united Africa. We often spent hours outside his restaurant, engaged in deep conversations about African politics and the continent's challenges. Ali's extensive travel across Africa and his involvement in the diamond industry gave him a unique perspective, enriching our talks with firsthand insights. The international clients he hosted—diamond buyers from around the world—added even more flavor to our conversations.

One day, Ali invited me to explore more of Johannesburg, an opportunity I eagerly accepted. He guided me through the bustling neighborhoods of Hillbrow and Braamfontein, areas known for their dense high-rise buildings and lively energy. While Hillbrow had a notorious reputation for high crime—stabbings, shootings, and robberies—Ali navigated the streets with ease, giving me a local's view of its vibrant nightlife. Our destination was Summit, a strip club that left me astounded with its electric atmosphere and the stunning beauty of the women. With the exchange rate in my favor—one dollar converting to about 21 rand—my spending power felt limitless, and Summit quickly became a favorite spot.

Summit wasn't just a strip club—it was an experience. The women, who lived upstairs, offered additional services that provided a level of convenience and privacy, elevating the entire visit. It was hands down the most impressive club I'd ever been to, and it soon became a regular haunt.

On one of our visits, Ali introduced me to bitter kola, a traditional African seed known for its medicinal properties, particularly for enhancing male vitality. This discovery was just one of many that highlighted the depth of Ali's cultural knowledge, making each outing not only entertaining but also educational. Through these explorations and encounters, Johannesburg began to reveal its many layers—blending vibrant urban life with cultural richness, a hint of danger, and a unique charm that made my experience in the city captivating.

A Deeper Dive into Johannesburg's Realities

As I grew more accustomed to life in Johannesburg, I decided to extend my stay and approached my landlord about altering the rental agreement. She was a middle-aged Afrikaner woman, and after understanding my need for flexibility, she agreed to a month-to-month payment plan and even offered me a discount. This new arrangement gave me the financial breathing room I needed for my extended stay.

Living in Johannesburg exposed me to the intricate racial and economic dynamics of South Africa. It was both intriguing and unsettling to witness large white populations in Africa, particularly the Afrikaners, who, despite being only 5% of the population, controlled over 95% of the wealth. This stark disparity was visible throughout the city, with many Black South Africans living in shantytowns like Soweto and Alexandra, while the affluent white populations resided in the luxurious northern suburbs.

One place that exemplified this wealth divide was Sandton, known as Africa's richest square mile. My first visit there was eye-opening. The area's opulence and modern infrastructure reminded me of Beverly Hills. Mandela Square, surrounded by high-end restaurants that could rival Michelin-star establishments, highlighted the immense prosperity of this enclave.

Despite the uncomfortable wealth gap, a common sentiment among South Africans—both Black and white—was that Johannesburg's modern, sophisticated cityscape might not have been possible without the contributions of the white people there.

While I agreed with this perspective, it wasn't without controversy. It revealed the tangled history of tension, reliance, and the undeniable role different communities played in shaping the city. As I came to terms with these realities, Johannesburg unfolded before me—vibrant and full of life, yet marked by deep divisions. Each neighborhood I visited offered something new, expanding my understanding of South Africa and reshaping my views on the city's unique blend of histories and cultures.

Just hours earlier, I'd left a place backwards and primitive, and now, only seven hours later, I was standing in a city that pulsed with the energy of an American metropolis, yet I was still in Africa. Ghana had no real cultural pulse that I could tap into, but South Africa was a different beast entirely—its scene was raw, alive, gritty, and unfiltered, like stepping into 1990s Brooklyn. The air buzzed with something intense, and I knew I was diving headfirst into a world unknown, meeting people I never would have encountered if I hadn't taken the leap. The vibe was electric, and I was chasing it, ready for whatever came next.

Johannesburg's Diverse Black African Population

Johannesburg's appeal comes from its incredible diversity—not just in terms of race, but in the wide range of African diasporas it hosts. The city is a true melting pot, blending vibrant Indian communities, various groups of whites, and Africans from across the continent. This rich mix makes Johannesburg a dynamic hub for networking. The personal connections I've made stretch across Africa —from South Sudanese to Congolese to West Africans—each drawn to South Africa for better economic opportunities than what their home countries offer.

One encounter that sticks with me is with my Angolan friend, who didn't hold back in expressing her dislike for South Africans. She wasn't alone in this sentiment—many Africans who come here for work feel a disdain for the locals, even while seeking opportunities in their country. I began to see the tension more clearly after another experience, this time with an Afrikaner woman who treated a Zambian woman far better than she treated South Africans. She praised the Zambian's work ethic but dismissed local South Africans as lazy, reinforcing a divide that ran deeper than I'd realized.

This scenario reminded me of the racial dynamics in the United States, where Black Americans face discrimination while Africans and Caribbeans are favored by the societal majority—and even join forces with white Americans in their biases. Similarly, in South Africa, many Africans from other countries follow the same pattern, adopting the prejudices held by white South Africans against Black locals. They distance themselves from the locals and, in some cases, even contribute to the very racism that South Africans endure.

The parallels don't stop there. In Johannesburg, Coloureds—mixed-race individuals—act as a buffer, similar to Hispanics in the U.S. Though many Coloureds would be considered Black in America, here they fiercely cling to their distinct identity to maintain a social status above Black South Africans.

Thus, Johannesburg's racial hierarchy subtly unfolds: Whites at the top, followed by Coloureds, then other Africans, and native South Africans at the bottom. This stratification breeds divisions and creates a complex web of acceptance and exclusion within the Black community itself, where historical prejudices collide with new societal challenges.

As a Black American male, my presence in Johannesburg has been somewhat of an anomaly. The local admiration for and emulation of Black American culture has given me a unique advantage, making it easier to navigate this complex social landscape. This cultural connection has often placed me in a privileged position within the city's intricate social hierarchy, smoothing interactions and opening doors that might otherwise remain closed.

Navigating this place has been a real eye-opener, revealing the deep layers of race and society in a city as complex as Johannesburg. I've come to see just how ingrained these social hierarchies are in shaping people's interactions and opportunities. Being a Black American comes with a certain privilege and cultural currency I hadn't fully realized before. The admiration for Black American culture has opened doors for me that many locals don't have access to, giving me a kind of influence here that I wasn't expecting.

The Influence of Black American Culture in South Africa

To truly understand the influence of Black American culture in South Africa, you only need look at everyday life around the city. The impact is unmistakable, from fashion to language. The attire commonly seen on the streets reflects styles popularized by hip-hop and R&B artists, serving as a clear homage to these genres. Local vernacular is laced with American slang and mannerisms, a testament to the powerful appeal and widespread adoption of Black American cultural expressions. South Africans not only embrace this influence but also idolize Black American icons, seamlessly integrating them into their own cultural landscape.

But this admiration isn't without its layers. Unlike in other African countries, where jealousy toward Black Americans might be more obvious, the fascination here is more subtle. Some locals see Black Americans as coming from a place of privilege because of their U.S. background, and that can create a certain tension. Even in friendships, that sense of economic advantage can linger in the background, shaping how relationships unfold.

Black Americans traveling or moving to South Africa should be aware of these underlying dynamics. The admiration for Black American culture is sincere and widespread, but it exists alongside a subtle awareness of perceived privilege. Understanding this layer of complexity is crucial for navigating social interactions thoughtfully and authentically. In South Africa, as in much of Africa, admiration, emulation, and economic reality coexist, shaping a unique cultural exchange that is both enriching and challenging for the expatriate experience.

However, my Black American heritage opened doors in unexpected ways, helping me forge connections with various communities, including West Africans from Ghana and Nigeria. Bonding over shared experiences of places like Labadi Beach, we quickly built a sense of camaraderie. But beneath these friendships lay a darker reality. Many of them were involved in illicit activities— specifically, elaborate dating scams targeting lonely, older women from the U.S., Europe, and Asia. The scale of these scams was shocking, with single victims losing as much as $35,000. Despite their generous offers to pay for my accommodations with their ill-gotten wealth, I knew better than to accept.

Outside of the West African community, my background also gave me access to Johannesburg's underground networks within the Coloured population. Many had connections to crime, but they were equally fascinated by my story as a Black American. One particularly memorable encounter was with a Coloured woman who, after realizing I was Black American, kissed me on the cheek and said, "I'm so sorry for what your people go through." It was a deeply personal moment that left a lasting impression on me.

This sense of connection extended beyond the Coloured community. In Johannesburg, I was viewed differently than in America, where Black men often face negative stereotypes as thugs or gangsters. Here, toughness and resilience were admired. Instead of being judged or feared, I was respected for qualities that are maligned back home. People recognized not just physical strength but the resilience of surviving against the odds. This made me realize that our voice, shaped by the American struggle, resonates far beyond our borders. It's not just the voice of the American ghetto but of streets everywhere, where people fight to be heard.

Local gangsters and everyday citizens idolized Black Americans, with cultural icons like Tupac and Ice Cube painted on graffiti-covered walls in Johannesburg's toughest neighborhoods—symbols of a lifestyle both respected and emulated. Moving through the city, I saw how Black culture had left its mark, shaping how people expressed themselves and navigated their realities. This experience deepened my understanding of how cultural identities collide, blending admiration with a profound connection to a world far from their own. It challenged how I viewed my identity and its far-reaching influence.

Homicides Lurk on Every Corner

Johannesburg is a city where the threat of armed robbery and violence looms on every street, a constant shadow over daily life. With over 2,400 murders each year and the highest rates of rape in the world, the city is grappling with staggering crime levels. Cash-in-transit operations are a particularly striking example of the city's volatile nature—entire blocks are cordoned off, guarded by heavily armed security personnel wielding assault rifles to deter brazen thieves. I vividly recall stumbling into one of these high-security zones. A security officer with his rifle at the ready quickly assessed my presence and, after a tense moment, allowed me to pass without harm. On another occasion, I witnessed a security guard chase after a thief who had snatched a woman's phone, only to be met with gunfire. The bullet narrowly missed his head, knocking off his hat, leaving him shaken and sprawled on the ground, visibly shocked by his near-death experience.

The Central Business District (CBD) is a hotbed of criminal activity, notorious for its unforgiving streets by day and a near-warzone atmosphere after dark. Hillbrow, with its towering high-rise buildings crammed with tens of thousands of undocumented immigrants, many from Zimbabwe, is infamous for its lawlessness.

My visits to these areas were marked by extreme caution, and I made a strict rule never to wander at night unless I was sure of my destination. Casual exploration in these parts could mean walking into real danger, a risk I wasn't willing to take.

Adding to the city's dangers are ongoing taxi and Uber wars that have escalated from verbal confrontations to lethal battles. Traditional taxi drivers, enraged by Uber's encroachment, have resorted to violent measures, including murder, to defend their territory. On more than one occasion, I found myself stranded as Uber drivers refused to enter certain areas, fearing for their lives. They would often ask me to walk blocks away from taxi ranks, ensuring that their arrival wouldn't trigger a deadly confrontation.

Within Johannesburg's diverse communities, the Zulus command a particular level of caution. Known for their fierce pride, rooted in historical victories against British and other European forces, some Zulus carry a confrontational demeanor that can escalate quickly. More than once, a disagreement turned tense with the chilling threat, "I'm a Zulu, I will shoot you," reminding me of the deep-seated tensions simmering just beneath the surface.

Even in affluent areas like Sandton, often called the richest square mile in Africa, safety is an illusion. Criminals, blending in with the luxurious surroundings, conduct swift, violent crimes—carjackings, muggings, and kidnappings are everyday occurrences. In these wealthy enclaves, residents fortify their homes with high fences, electric barriers, and private security teams. These defenses reflect the pervasive fear that even wealth cannot dispel.

The big difference here, though, is that in America, Black men are singled out as the primary targets, but in Johannesburg, no one is exempt—everyone is a potential target, regardless of their background.

It was amazing to see the diversity of African populations. I met people from Congo, Tanzania, Swaziland, and many other places, each sharing their unique stories about life across the continent. It felt like I was learning about Africa firsthand through their experiences. I was welcomed like family, and for the first time, I felt at home—a complete difference from Ghana, where there was no sense of solidarity. Here, Pan-Africanism seemed real, and I finally felt like I'd caught up with the shadow I'd been chasing all along.

Even though the city was vibrant and full of new things to discover every day, the level of crime in Johannesburg was unlike anything I'd ever seen. The streets were treacherous mirroring the worst inner cities in America. In Ghana, the biggest worry was malaria, but Johannesburg forced me to rely on street smarts again. Shootouts and armed robberies were a daily concern, and I had to blend in with the crowd, avoiding any hint of wealth. Looking too well-off was a risk, so I learned to adopt a more rugged, almost gangster-like appearance to keep attention off me and staying under the radar.

Between the Roars and the Cradle of Mankind

Sometimes the relentless pace of the city called for an escape, and I found solace in the untouched wilderness of South Africa's famed safaris—a significant departure from the urban sprawl. Known for offering some of the best safari experiences in the world, South Africa invites both the cautious and the bold to explore its vast landscapes, whether from the safety of caged trucks or, for the daring, behind the wheel of a rental car, getting closer to the wild.

On one of these much-needed getaways, I called an Uber and asked the driver for a recommendation. He suggested Lion's Park in the Cradle of Humankind, located in the Northwest Province. It was fascinating how just a short drive from the city could transport you to a place that felt like the dawn of time. Upon arrival, the driver offered to wait while I joined the safari tour—Johannesburg felt close, but this wilderness seemed a world away.

As the safari truck arrived, I noticed something interesting: I was the only Black person among the tourists. It reminded me of the differences I'd seen in the city, but out here in the open savannah, it felt more pronounced. We set off into the wild, and the sense of adventure was undeniable. One of the first sights was a pride of lions, notorious for a tragic incident years ago when a woman fell victim to their power. Today, they lounged by a waterhole, calm and indifferent, as if their violent past was far behind them.

The safari unfolded like a live-action scene from Animal Planet. Cheetahs darted in the distance, wild dogs prowled the outskirts, and we spotted warthogs scurrying alongside vigilant meerkats and towering ostriches. But it was the elusive leopard that truly captured everyone's attention. Revered and feared by locals, this predator's cunning and agility required isolation to prevent escape.

A strange moment occurred during the tour—a Middle Eastern man, perhaps caught up in the excitement, began growling at the caged leopard. The animal's eyes flashed with ferocity, a sharp reminder of the thin line between human bravado and the unrestrained power of nature.

After the safari, the experience shifted to a more hands-on interaction. I had the chance to play with baby lions, their playful antics masking the lethal potential of their kind. Their rough tongues, designed for shearing flesh, licked at my hands, and I marveled at how easily these cute creatures could one day strip flesh from bone. Feeding giraffes, on the other hand, was a more gentle experience. Their graceful movements and soft interactions were a peaceful contrast to the ferocity of the lions.

Amid all the excitement, one observation lingered: the safari was operated and predominantly owned by white entrepreneurs, while local Black Africans served as drivers and guides. It reflected the ongoing reality where Africa's natural treasures are managed and monetized by those outside the local community—a modern reflection of colonial legacies that persist today.

As the sun dipped below the horizon, painting the sky in hues of fiery orange and deep purple, I suddenly remembered my Uber driver, who had waited throughout my adventure. His irritation had softened into resigned patience, and I apologized, offering him extra compensation for his time. As we headed back to the gritty reality of Johannesburg, my mind remained lost in the wild, still wandering the untamed landscapes of the safari.

I couldn't shake the image of that look on the leopard's face. It was eerie, unsettling even, and I noticed the safari guides showed them the most respect out of all the animals. Known as a man-eater, the leopard was kept separate from the others, and it made me wonder if they were the true kings of the jungle after all. There was something about their presence, something untamed and commanding, that set them apart from the rest.

Unexpected Journey into Soweto

I couldn't claim to have seen South Africa without visiting Soweto. During one of my random Uber rides to the mall, I learned that my driver hailed from there. He was a lively, witty man in his 40s, brimming with energy. When he found out I had never visited Soweto, his enthusiasm was immediate. "You've never been to Soweto? Then you haven't really seen South Africa," he declared. I agreed to his offer to show me around, feeling excited about this spontaneous detour.

As we drove away from the bustling cityscape, the environment began to transform. The towering buildings gave way to smaller, single-family homes interspersed with shanties. Contrary to my expectations, shaped by media portrayals, I found the area cleaner than the inner city and the people noticeably more welcoming. It was a refreshing contradiction to the grim narratives often presented about historically Black neighborhoods.

Our first stop was at the iconic Soweto Towers, where we snapped pictures, surrounded by colorful murals. From there, we headed to Nelson Mandela's house, now a tourist destination attracting visitors from all over the world. As we strolled through the streets, I noticed groups of white tourists on bikes. Rather than engaging with the history and culture, it felt like they were watching the locals from a distance, as if they were on a human safari. Their presence gave the whole scene an unsettling vibe, as though the people of Soweto were on display rather than being respected as part of the community's living history. Throughout the tour, my driver shared deeper, darker aspects of Soweto's past. He revealed that the township wasn't just designed to house Black people—it was strategically planned for suppression.

The roads and houses were laid out in a way that allowed for easy military access, with the sinister purpose of bombing the area in case of uprisings. This chilling reality cast a long shadow over the vibrant streets, a reminder of the resilience and enduring spirit of Soweto's residents, who thrived despite oppressive designs.

This impromptu journey not only debunked many misconceptions but also enriched my understanding of South Africa's intricate history. As we headed back to Johannesburg, I felt a deeper connection to the country, eager to explore more of its distinctions and legacies.

Quick Stop in Botswana / Lifelessness and Precious Stones

Back in my Johannesburg apartment, I was hit by a nagging realization—my visa was about to expire, and I needed to leave the country to reset it. Looking for nearby options, my choices narrowed to Maputo, Tanzania, or Gaborone, Botswana. Gaborone, being the closest, seemed like the easiest choice.

While explaining my plan to my neighbors, my Ghanaian friend boldly offered to pull off a a quick dating scam to cover my expenses. I laughed it off, assured him I had things under control, and focused on planning the trip. After some research, I booked a stay at the I Towers in downtown Gaborone and secured my bus ticket for my first road trip through Africa.

The bus was packed with travelers, and the air buzzed with anticipation—though mine was likely the strongest. The five-hour journey cost around $20, and as we left the city behind, the landscape shifted into vast stretches of countryside. Just when I thought the trip couldn't get more surreal, I saw something I'd only dreamed of: my first wild elephant, casually strolling down the road, with herds of zebras grazing in the distance. "There's an elephant!" I shouted, unable to contain my excitement, but the locals barely reacted, giving me amused looks. For them, this was routine. For me, it was pure magic.

Crossing the border was uneventful, and soon we were approaching Gaborone. The difference from Johannesburg was immediate and undeniable. Gaborone lacked the energy, the hustle, and the chaos of Jozi. Instead, it was quiet—almost too quiet, as if the city was waiting for something to stir it awake.

Checking into my room at the I Towers, I was struck by how luxurious it was—more opulent than anywhere I had stayed. As the tallest building in Botswana, it stood out against the subdued city below. Looking out at the quiet streets, the difference between the luxury inside and the lifeless city outside felt surreal.

The next morning, I set off to explore, following my routine of walking around and trying local restaurants, but Gaborone left me underwhelmed. The food was decent, but the city had no spark. It was clean, orderly, but lacked any real energy. Even the people I encountered were polite but without the vibrant personalities I'd come to expect in South Africa.

With taxis scarce, I found myself walking everywhere. As I wandered through the fancier parts of town, I noticed how different the atmosphere felt—luxury hotels, polished storefronts, and quiet cafes. It wasn't long before I overheard a conversation that caught my attention: local African leaders in deep discussions with white investors from Canada. As I listened in, it became clear that Botswana, rich with diamond reserves, was being carved up by these foreign investors, with local leaders willingly offering up their resources. The dynamic was unsettling—foreign control over local wealth, echoing the old patterns of colonialism.

Hoping to shake off those thoughts, I spent the evening at the hotel bar. There, I met three women and we shared drinks, but the highlight of the night was the bartender. His friendly demeanor and generosity, even gifting me a bottle to take back to my room, brought some lightness to the otherwise dull atmosphere.

Despite these brief moments of amusement, Gaborone felt stifling. The lack of vitality weighed on me. The city felt lifeless, its energy drained by the resources it exported to the West. The people, like the city, seemed to be running on empty. Disappointed and restless, I decided to cut my visit short. Packing my bags, I left Gaborone's stillness behind, eager to return to the vibrant chaos of Jozi, knowing I wouldn't look back.

Botswana was a lifeless country with no draw or personality. The only thing I noticed was that it served as a grocery store for white men to get diamonds, and the Africans there were more than delighted to help them.

A Return to Jozi / Recharged by the Pulse of South Africa

Relief washed over me as I stepped off the bus back in South Africa, the vibrant energy of the city instantly lifting my spirits. The familiar hustle of the taxi stand greeted me, and soon enough, a young Pedi man in his mid-20s flagged me down with a wide grin. His excitement grew when he found out I was black American, and without hesitation, he cranked up the music, the beats pulsing through the car and sped off into the lively streets. He told me that to survive here, you had to be tough, illustrating his point by casually pulling a pistol from beneath his seat. The mix of warmth and danger was an intense reminder of South Africa's reality. Despite the jarring moment, his easygoing nature and the thumping music made for an oddly enjoyable ride—an intriguing, spirited welcome back to Jozi that I couldn't help but appreciate.

As we neared my apartment, I was surprised to see Ali lounging outside, his face lighting up with amusement as I stepped out of the taxi. "Why are you back so soon?" he chuckled, his smile teasing. I explained that Botswana had been underwhelming, lifeless compared to Johannesburg's constant buzz. "That's because Botswana is what the Africans built. Here, the whites built this," he remarked, his words laced with a cynical truth that stayed with me long after our conversation ended.

Once inside my apartment, a familiar sense washed over me. The textures, colors, and atmosphere of the room enveloped me in a welcome embrace. Grateful for the extended visa that allowed me to stay longer, I took a moment to reflect on my brief time away. The stillness of Gaborone felt like a different world from the constant energy of Johannesburg, where every street buzzed with life. Feeling recharged and ready to dive back into the city's vibrant rhythm, I remembered why Jozi had such a grip on me. The lackluster adventure in Botswana quickly faded as I prepared to embrace the rich experiences waiting in South Africa—a traveler renewed, eager for whatever lay ahead.

Jozi's Dating scene

Exploring the dating scene in South Africa has been eye-opening —vastly different from anywhere I've known. As a Black American man, I've found this country to be a social haven. The respect and admiration I've encountered here stand in sharp relief to the challenging realities in the United States, where Black men are frequently undervalued due to systemic issues. It's a sobering reminder of the disparity in cultural attitudes, and unfortunately, many Black Americans never venture far enough to experience this shift, where their identity is not only acknowledged but celebrated.

The allure of Black American men here goes beyond mere curiosity—there's genuine respect and admiration that shapes every interaction. Whether in vibrant clubs pulsing with Gqom music or at cozy cafes scattered across the city, the reception has been overwhelmingly positive. One afternoon at a trendy café, I experienced this firsthand. A stunning Zimbabwean woman, initially dining with a wealthy white man, shifted her attention toward me the moment she heard my American accent.

Her interest was immediate and undeniable as the man she had been with quickly faded into the background. We connected easily, our conversation flowing naturally despite our different backgrounds. This moment highlighted a broader reality in South Africa: a strong fascination and admiration for Black American men.

The social scene offers countless opportunities to meet African women from across the continent. I've connected with people from Swaziland, Congo, Kenya, and beyond. These encounters offer more than just casual exchanges; they deepen my understanding of the incredible cultural diversity that defines Africa, making my time here even more enriching.

However, amid this vibrant scene, another phenomenon emerges—the presence of "Slay Queens." These impeccably dressed women, often seen in high-end venues, come from shantytowns or ghettos but are drawn to the allure of "blessers," wealthy benefactors who fund their luxurious lifestyles. This highlights the economic inequalities in South Africa, where beauty and charm can become paths to social mobility in a society that rewards ambition.

Nigerian men are also influential players in the nightlife, known for their generosity and reputation for lavish spending, making them particularly popular with women. Their presence adds another layer to the club scene, where status and wealth shape social interactions, shifting the balance of power with each night out.

Maboneng District – Africa's Black Wall Street

The connections I made beyond the dating scene in South Africa were equally compelling, offering new layers of experience. The entrepreneurial spirit in Johannesburg was particularly inspiring, driven by dynamic energy and creativity. Whether stepping into lively social settings or attending elegant cultural events, the city's vibrancy felt immersive and inviting.

One of the most memorable moments was attending an opera performance by a friend who is an exceptionally talented singer. The event radiated elegance, showcasing her incredible vocal skills and the city's rich cultural diversity. The fashion shows I attended exploded with color and design, reflecting South Africa's innovative artistic spirit. These shows celebrated creativity, revealing that fashion is as much about craftsmanship as it is about aesthetics.

Dining in upscale areas like Sandton and Pretoria revealed another side of South African society. In these affluent settings, conversations often turned to the country's disparities, with many drawing parallels to the global inequalities seen in places like the United States. The social and economic divides, while different in context, had their own local nuances.

Academically, my curiosity was sparked by seminars at prestigious institutions like the University of Witwatersrand, or 'Wits' for short, and the AFDA institution. These discussions were intellectually invigorating, akin to a think tank, grounded in African perspectives. The students and scholars I encountered engaged in deep, critical conversations about international affairs, offering fresh viewpoints on Africa's role in global discourse.

However, in Maboneng, I truly felt the heartbeat of Johannesburg's networking scene. This neighborhood was a hub of connections, filled with vibrant restaurants, bars, and the lively Market on Main, transforming every Sunday into a bustling space of commerce and culture. Entrepreneurs from various fields gathered, offering everything from handmade crafts to exotic foods, creating a perfect setting for anyone wanting to tap into the city's entrepreneurial spirit. My camera became a tool for opening conversations, turning snapshots into meaningful interactions. It was here that I made some of my most remarkable connections, including royalty and dignitaries—among them, a princess whose father was a sitting president.

Maboneng was not just a business center but a cultural sanctuary, showcasing the potential of Africa's Black communities. It surpassed affluent Black areas in the U.S., like Baldwin Hills and Prince George's County, in terms of vibrancy and success. Maboneng represents the most dynamic and prosperous Black community I've encountered globally. But with success also comes challenges—the drive for progress here can sometimes lead to rivalry and sabotage, revealing the complications that arise with rapid development in thriving Black communities.

From my extensive travels, I can confidently say that Johannesburg, especially Maboneng, stands out as one of the most vibrant Black communities worldwide. The city's ability to connect people across social groups, along with endless networking opportunities among innovative entrepreneurs, creates a compelling environment. As a Black American, I didn't just find acceptance here—I found a sense of belonging and the chance to thrive in a truly global setting. Johannesburg isn't just a place to live—it's a stage where the world comes together in meaningful ways.

I had never truly felt appreciated until this moment, and the phrase "go where you're appreciated, not tolerated" finally resonated with me. This wasn't a one–off experience—every Black American man I saw traveling here was treated the same. It wasn't just about the stunning beauty of the women, but the effortless, cool vibes they brought with them. In South Africa, for the first time, the Black American man can feel what it truly means to be wanted, to be valued, in a way that goes beyond tolerance. It was a feeling impossible to experience in America, a place where Black American men are hated.

Vibrancy Amid Insidiousness

Amid the vibrant allure of Maboneng, a subtle yet unsettling undercurrent ran beneath the surface. While the rich cultural experiences and bustling energy of the community were captivating, I remained focused on observing the less visible dynamics at play. As I navigated the eclectic crowds at Market on Main, I noticed several individuals who seemed out of place—whites from America and Europe, alongside African Americans, some conspicuously dressed in overly traditional African attire, adorned with elaborate necklaces and tattoos.

One encounter at Market on Main stood out, offering deeper insight into what might lie beneath the cultural display. I approached a Black woman whose attire was theatrical—an almost exaggerated celebration of African heritage, complete with bold accessories and intricate tattoos. Her appearance seemed to attract attention, particularly from expatriates and   Black Americans, who might be drawn to what appeared to be an authentic expression of African pride.

As we engaged in conversation, a white woman approached and joined us, sparking an abrupt shift in the interaction. The Black woman quickly distanced herself, as though they were complete strangers. This sudden change felt orchestrated and revealed a deeper layer to the encounter.

It reminded me of similar tactics I had witnessed in Ghana, where individuals donning pro-Black attire weren't simply celebrating their culture but were sometimes part of a larger scheme to attract and monitor tourists and expatriates.

The presence of these individuals in heavily frequented areas like Market on Main highlighted a potential risk for Black Americans involved in business or social interactions in Johannesburg. In some cases, pro-Black attire can be more than just an expression of cultural pride—it can serve as a tool for drawing in certain people for scrutiny. This realization heightened my awareness of the need to stay vigilant and discerning, as not all cultural displays are as innocent as they seem.

Meanwhile, another troubling issue unfolded at a governmental level. Despite Maboneng's economic growth and endless potential, the expected government focus on public safety was conspicuously absent. The area was becoming overrun by criminals, yet there was little police presence. The few security guards in place, armed only with whips, were largely ineffective. This neglect seemed intentional, part of a broader strategy to stifle the area's development by fostering fear and insecurity.

This revelation cast a shadow over the vibrancy of Maboneng, revealing a deeper narrative. The government's allowance of criminal elements to thrive threatened not only the community's safety but also its future as a beacon of cultural and economic growth in Johannesburg. What should have been a flourishing enclave was now at risk of being sabotaged by those who stood to gain from its decline.

The Maboneng District was the most remarkable Black community I'd ever encountered, even more than Prince George's County in Maryland. The concentration of Black intellectuals, politicians, and creatives in one space was remarkable. Sundays at Market on Main showcased this abundance, thriving with a vibrant energy that made it a cultural epicenter. Yet, with such success, it was clear that not everyone wanted to see it flourish. As I watched the white visitors, the hatred in their eyes was impossible to explain. It felt as if they couldn't stand to witness Black excellence thriving. A sign that once read "Maboneng is for Black people" had been crossed out, now reading "Maboneng is for all people"—an insidious change.

Sexuality Throughout Africa

Exploring Johannesburg after spending time in Ghana revealed striking differences in public expressions of sexuality. In South Africa, LGBT visibility is unmistakably more prominent, a distinct contrast to other African nations I'd visited. Johannesburg, much like Atlanta in the United States, serves as a beacon of acceptance, and both cities would be considered black gay capitals.

In Johannesburg's nightclubs and social spots, it's common to see men in feminine attire and makeup, as well as women openly in relationships. This acceptance extends into everyday life, with waitstaff confidently wearing clothing traditionally associated with the opposite sex. The city's inclusive atmosphere makes it a hub for gay Africans, mirroring Atlanta's role in fostering a welcoming environment. Many gay South Africans recognize Atlanta's reputation and express a desire to experience its celebrated lifestyle.

This striking level of acceptance and openness in Johannesburg extremely differs with what I've encountered in places like Ghana and Botswana, where gay expressions are suppressed, if not outright persecuted. For instance, during a visit to Rosebank Mall, a friend pointed out a young, feminine man rumored to be romantically involved with a government minister. This level of open discussion and visibility of LGBT individuals was unheard of in all other parts of Black Africa and the Caribbean, where severe social and legal repercussions for same-sex interactions prevail. Such actions in other African countries would lead to death.

This dramatic difference prompted me to reflect on the profound impact that white supremacy has had on African societies and others around the world with significant black populations. It becomes apparent that in countries with minimal or no direct influence from white politics, LGBT culture among black communities is almost nonexistent. For example, in nations like Jamaica, Ghana, Congo, and Haiti—where indigenous cultural norms have remained relatively untouched by Western interference—the presence and acceptance of LGBT identities are virtually absent.

Conversely, in regions that have experienced extensive historical and ongoing interference from white populations—through colonialism or cultural globalization—there is a noticeable shift toward greater acceptance and visibility of gay communities. Countries like Colombia, Brazil, and the United States, which boast significant black populations and close proximity to white influence, show a much higher level of visibility and acceptance of LGBT individuals. This correlation strongly suggests that the cultural norms regarding sexuality in black communities are significantly shaped by the level and nature of white political and cultural intrusion.

Furthermore, international relations and aid dynamics play a significant role in this cultural shift. Countries like the United States have been known to condition their aid on the recipient countries' acceptance and promotion of LGBTQ rights. This form of cultural imposition suggests that financial support comes with strings attached, pushing nations to adopt social policies that align with values promoted by white countries.

Additionally, my visits to private schools in Africa—managed or funded by white organizations—revealed a curriculum heavily focused on promoting concepts like gender fluidity and feminism. These teachings, differ from traditional educational content in African education & highlights a deliberate effort to reshape the cultural landscape under the guise of education.

European cultural norms have significantly influenced South Africa's social dynamics, particularly regarding taboo sexual practices and the fetishization of Black males. The presence of white Europeans in South Africa has fostered a more open attitude toward unconventional sexual expressions. This openness has eroticized Black figures, fueling a culture of exotic and overly sexualized encounters. These shifts toward liberal sexual practices reflect not only the personal inclinations of these residents but also a deeper integration of European sexual norms into the local society. This cultural assimilation has profound implications, particularly the rise of Black feminine men, which corresponds with a decrease in traditional warrior figures in the community.

Feminism in Africa

Discussing gender roles and feminism in South Africa reveals dynamics similar to those shaped by white political structures elsewhere, although the degree of feminism among South African women is milder than that in the U.S. or Europe. In South Africa, Black women often receive workforce preference over Black men, resulting in perceptions of Black men as less competent. This view mirrors dynamics in the United States, where economic opportunities often favor Black American women over their male counterparts, shaping perceptions within their communities. In both contexts, these shifts in traditional gender dynamics, driven by predominantly white-owned businesses, erode family structures and diminish respect for Black men. This weakens the cohesion of Black family units, paralleling the societal shifts observed in American Black communities.

In contrast, in places like Ghana, where men often dominate the workforce, traditional gender roles are more respected, and men are held in higher regard. This suggests that when Black men hold economic power, they command greater respect and authority. Additionally, many African women outside South Africa reject Western-style feminism, preferring traditional roles and seeking leadership from men. This highlights a significant cultural divergence from Western feminist ideologies and indicates a strong adherence to traditional values across much of Africa.

These observations suggest that where there is direct white influence, feminism is actively promoted; in its absence, it is largely absent. This relationship between economic independence, cultural values, and gender perceptions shapes societal roles and attitudes toward feminism and gender equality across various African contexts.

South Africa's Economy

Exploring the economic landscape of South Africa reveals why this nation is a more appealing destination for Black Americans considering relocation than other African countries. South Africa's financial systems provide a familiarity and accessibility that significantly ease the transition for those used to the structured economic environments of first-world countries. In contrast to many other African nations, where purchasing property or a vehicle requires upfront cash payments—creating significant barriers for those without substantial savings—South Africa offers more flexible financing options. In South Africa, one can finance a house or car similarly to the United States, utilizing structured payment plans and credit systems that accommodate diverse financial situations.

This flexibility also extends to various business transactions, making South Africa an economically viable option for those without large amounts of cash on hand. This ease of doing business in South Africa is notably different from that in places like Ghana, which is often promoted as a prime relocation spot for Black Americans. Ghana's deep-rooted cultural significance and historical richness make it an alluring destination for many, but its economic structure presents significant challenges.

The country lacks a robust banking network and reliable credit facilities, leading to a predominantly cash-based economy that excludes those lacking substantial liquid assets. Additionally, Ghana lacks sympathetic business practices for Black individuals, and fairness in financial dealings is frequently missing. Even for those who manage to navigate the deadly prevalence of malaria, financial hurdles can be overwhelming.

In South Africa, a more supportive environment exists where Black pride is prevalent, and businesses frequently extend special considerations or deals to Black individuals. This fosters a sense of community and support while easing the path for Black Americans looking to establish themselves financially. These dynamics render South Africa a more appealing and viable option for those seeking stability and fairness in economic and business dealings.

Moreover, the quality of infrastructure and the clarity of financial dealings in South Africa make it a standout option. An illustrative incident occurred when a street vendor in Johannesburg's Central Business District chased me down to return excess change I had mistakenly paid. This level of honesty, combined with the practice of fixed pricing in stores—unlike in other parts of Africa, where prices can be arbitrary and haggling is common—demonstrates a system of fairness and transparency that aligns closely with American expectations.

These experiences highlight how easily Black Americans can integrate into South African society. The country's comparable financial structures, along with the fairness and predictability of its market practices, make South Africa a more attractive option than other African nations. The financial environment facilitates smoother transitions for newcomers and provides a stable foundation for those looking to invest and establish their financial roots in a new country.

Loadshedding

Load shedding in South Africa is a significant issue, with power outages sometimes lasting half the day, mirroring the energy struggles seen in Ghana. This challenge fosters community bonding, as people gather outside their homes and in the streets, united by the inconvenience. These gatherings become vibrant forums for debate, covering critiques of government policies and conspiracy theories.

Conversations consistently return to a consensus: the government's systematic oppression stifles prosperity among the populace, with threads of white supremacy woven into these policies. While the impact of load shedding is widespread, clear disparities emerge: affluent white neighborhoods often have resources and infrastructure to mitigate its worst effects, while predominantly Black areas suffer disproportionately.

This divide highlights ingrained inequalities and fuels growing discontent among the populace, who view these outages as another manifestation of a broader scheme to keep them disenfranchised.

The street dialogue, infused with frustration and insightful critique, paints a vivid portrait of a society grappling with the chains of historical and ongoing injustice, where the struggle for power—both literal and metaphorical—shapes the daily lives of its citizens.

Healthcare

The healthcare system in South Africa is remarkably accessible and efficient, featuring some of the best medical professionals in the world. During my stay, I experienced firsthand the high level of care provided, adeptly catering to both traditional and modern medical needs with exceptional ease.

After an injury that impaired my mobility, a visit to a public clinic saw me quickly assessed by a doctor who referred me to a surgeon. The consultation revealed that surgery wasn't necessary, and I was provided with a doctor's note that was promptly faxed and emailed to my healthcare providers in America. The process was seamless, and the cost was minimal—no insurance was needed, and the option to pay out-of-pocket made the experience hassle-free. This sharply differed from the American healthcare system, where navigating hospital visits can lead to exorbitant debts and possible discrimination.

South Africa's medical amenities and infrastructure support sophisticated procedures, highlighted by the fact that the first successful open-heart surgery was performed in Cape Town. This capability ensures that residents and visitors alike have access to first-world medical services.

Moreover, my proximity to medical facilities proved to be a major advantage. When I contracted a virus, I was able to walk to a nearby clinic and see a doctor at a private practice. The doctor quickly prescribed antibacterial pills—something that would have required a lengthy and expensive hospital visit in the United States.

Aside from conventional medicine, I also explored traditional healing with the help of a Sangoma, a highly respected traditional healer in South Africa. When a severe ailment left me unable to walk, a friend recommended I consult with her. She visited my apartment, assessed my condition, and returned the next day with a remedy—a large bottle of bitter herbal concoction. After a few days of following her treatment, I experienced a remarkable recovery. This introduction to traditional healing not only aided my recovery but deepened my appreciation for South Africa's rich cultural heritage, adding a magical layer to my journey.

The blend of advanced medical infrastructure and deeply respected traditional practices makes South Africa's healthcare system uniquely accommodating. It stands out as a leading destination for those seeking both comprehensive and culturally enriched medical care.

Accepted On Cloud 9

In South Africa, cannabis is legal and boasts some of the world's best strains, such as Durban Poison. My experiences with cannabis enriched my social life, thanks to a nearby Zimbabwean supplier. Friends from Ghana and Nigeria often shared their stashes, making our gatherings lively with kush and music. Many of my female friends also smoked, and we spent hours sharing music and engaging in deep conversations. These moments revealed the intricate perspectives of the people I met.

One incident truly made me feel accepted. While enjoying a smoke outside, a police officer approached and asked, "Why are you smoking weed in front of us?" He playfully snatched the joint, adding, "without letting me hit it first." This was a refreshing change from the hostile encounters I'd faced with racist officers back home, making South Africa feel more like home in a genuinely comforting way.

Sanitation

Reflecting on my time in South Africa, I noticed a significant difference in sanitation compared to Ghana. South Africa's well-maintained streets, complete with gutters and sidewalks, present a far more structured environment than those in Accra and many West African cities. One key factor for Black Americans considering relocation is the advanced home amenities available in South Africa. Homes typically feature functional toilets and reliable hot water, offering a level of cleanliness often absent in Ghanaian households. Public facilities in South Africa, including restaurants and stores, are equipped with proper hand-washing stations that include soap—luxuries that are often lacking in many parts of West Africa.

This difference in sanitation is crucial, as poor hygiene can lead to diseases such as malaria, cholera, and typhoid, prevalent in many African nations. South Africa has taken proactive steps to mitigate these health risks, which Ghana has yet to implement. Moreover, hygiene is more heavily emphasized in South Africa compared to other regions of Africa. For instance, in many countries outside South Africa, it's common for people to eat with their hands from communal plates without proper hand-washing. While culturally normal, this practice poses a hygiene risk, especially given that soap and hot water are scarce in many areas. For Black Americans, these practices can be concerning, as they may be more susceptible to illnesses stemming from unfamiliar hygiene habits. South Africa's emphasis on sanitation and personal hygiene renders it a safer and more appealing destination for those mindful of health while traveling in Africa.

It became clear to me during my time in South Africa that feminism was virtually unheard of across Africa—except here. With a sizable white population and direct influence, feminism and homosexuality thrived, while in neighboring countries, these ideas were non-existent. The difference was unmistakable, showing just how deeply white influence shaped these movements. The more I observed, the more this connection stood out as undeniable.

Even with Apartheid still raging in South Africa, something unsettling caught my attention. Every time I saw Black people suffering, there was a Jewish person nearby, telling them to stop complaining— because the Holocaust was worse. At first, I thought this was only a tactic used against Black Americans, but here I was, in one of the worlds most oppressed and struggling communities, listening to a white woman spew the same rhetoric. It hit me hard: the Jews had not only cornered the market on suffering but had positioned themselves as the ultimate shield, deflecting Black people's cries for justice and minimizing their pain. They had become the perfect buffer in our global fight for freedom

Reflections on Gauteng

Johannesburg is a city marked by vivid differences and complex dynamics. Embracing it requires an intricate dance of pleasure intertwined with glaring societal challenges. The city presents boundless networking opportunities, seamless integration, and an environment strikingly similar to America, making the prospect of moving there feel almost destined. Yet, Johannesburg is not without profound issues—there is a new apartheid, where just 5 percent of the white population owns 95 percent of the wealth, high crime rates persist, and economic disparities create a troubling picture.

Despite pervasive racism, Black Americans discover a unique advantage here. The locals' deep understanding of white supremacy fosters a bond, creating an emotional and spiritual connection less common in other African nations, where viewing whites as gods can be disheartening. The housing market is surprisingly accessible, with month-to-month payments for luxurious apartments around $800, providing a slice of Beverly Hills-style living at a fraction of the cost. This financial accessibility, along with fixed pricing and exemplary medical facilities, ensures a low-stress environment that fosters not just survival but thriving.

Enhancing Johannesburg's allure is its reputation for boasting the most beautiful and captivating Black women in the world. The city's sexual openness amplifies its appeal, offering exhilarating and liberating experiences unmatched elsewhere. Moreover, the women here display a unique appreciation for Black American men, more than I've encountered in any other country. This affection provides a sense of belonging absent in the United States, enriching interactions and deepening cultural engagement.

Moreover, the breathtaking wildlife and the persistence of traditional cultures infuse everyday life with a sense of magic and mystery. However, frequent load shedding and power outages serve as a constant reminder that, despite some American familiarity, you're still very much in Africa, grappling with unpredictable infrastructure. At times, the city's vibrant pulse is disrupted by violent riots, reflecting the government's complex entanglements with global powers. High crime rates add another layer of tension—not for the faint of heart—making it essential to remain vigilant at all times, as alertness is a daily necessity.

Living in Johannesburg is undeniably an adventure for Black Americans, offering a rich array of experiences, from gourmet cuisine and exquisite wineries to high-end shopping and navigating its challenging streets. It mirrors America in many ways but also diverges, providing a unique backdrop for those exploring a different facet of the African diaspora.

As much as Johannesburg feels like home, I know my journey through Africa is far from complete. With experiences in West and South Africa behind me, my next chapter beckons toward Central Africa. However, before diving deeper into the continent, a brief return to America awaits to reconnect with family and handle personal affairs. The adventure continues, promising deeper insights into the vast, diverse continent of Africa.

Journey Back, Eyes Forward

Returning to America after my extensive travels was bittersweet and jarring. The long journey back included a brief layover in Dubai, offering a clear difference from the familiar and unwelcome American cultural nuances that awaited me. Upon reentry, hearing the distinctly American accent and the abrasive tone of a particular white woman on the plane vividly reminded me of the horrors I had left behind and braced me for what was to come. The flight on the U.S. airline reminded me of the lack of amenities and comfort I had grown accustomed to on international carriers. Yet, the prospect of reuniting with family and friends lifted my spirits.

Once stateside, I wasted no time diving back into responsibilities. I managed to secure a new tenant for my property on the East Coast, streamlining what I hoped would be a quick transition back to everyday life. However, a visit to the hospital to address injuries sustained in Africa quickly soured my homecoming. The difference in healthcare was evident; the doctors were dismissive and rushed, reflecting the racial insensitivity I had temporarily escaped abroad.

My frustrations with the American healthcare system and constant racial undertones fueled my desire to plan my next departure. During this period, I reconnected with a friend from Zambia, Mwanza, a friend I met in Maboneng. She reached out about available land in Zambia—vast plots that were both large and affordable. Intrigued by her descriptions and the potential for a new beginning, I began researching Zambia, located in the heart of South Central Africa. She sent photos and videos of a 3-acre plot available for just $1,300, deepening my interest.

I spent about seven months at home, a time of preparation and reflection, increasingly aware of the oppressive racial dynamics that felt sharper after my time in Africa. The absence of police intimidation and the anonymity I experienced in Africa was replaced by overt racism and scrutiny upon my return. This adjustment was challenging. While it's a significant part of my story, I prefer not to dwell on these experiences, as my narrative focuses on my exploration of Africa.

Ready for the next chapter, I booked my flight, stopping in Dubai before heading to Lusaka, Zambia. Eager yet anxious, I looked forward to the adventures and insights this new African destination would hold. South Africa had felt like home in many ways, offering the best experience I'd had so far, but due to its crime and uncertainty, I wanted to see if there might be a place that felt a little safer and less hostile. Central Africa remained largely unexplored for me, and I felt the need to delve deeper into the continent before deciding where I might ultimately settle. This trip wasn't just another adventure; it was a continuation of my quest for a place of profound belonging and peace.

Lusaka, Zambia

Arriving in Zambia marked the start of an adventure that tested my endurance and flexibility. After a grueling 21-hour flight, I felt immediate relief upon spotting Mwanza at Kenneth Kaunda Airport, holding a sign with my name. However, that relief evaporated quickly as we stepped outside to face the daunting task of finding a taxi. Taxi fares were exorbitantly high, bordering on extortion. Despite Mwanza's insistence to resist the inflated rates, the sweltering 90-degree heat and my fatigue quickly eroded my patience. As taxis became scarce, we were compelled to walk nearly two miles with my luggage in tow, intensifying the ordeal.

After finally securing a taxi, the driver hesitated at the distance to our destination, Rufunsa Village, and instead dropped us at a bus station. There, we faced another hurdle: the bus wouldn't leave until nearly full, a common practice in Zambia to maximize profits. This policy led to a two-hour wait in a dimly lit station, a stark departure from the vibrant city life I was accustomed to. As night fell, the absence of city lights unveiled a stunning canvas of stars overhead, offering small solace amid the journey's growing frustrations. By the time we reached Rufunsa, my patience with the situation and Mwanza was wearing thin. I questioned her, "Didn't you plan this out?" as we faced another snag. The room we intended to stay in wasn't reserved, and once locals noticed a foreigner with bags, they jacked up the price. Exhausted, I reluctantly agreed to the inflated cost, desperate for rest.

Despite the tumultuous start, the tranquility of the Zambian night soothed my frayed nerves. After Mwanza's apologetic departure, I stepped outside under a thatched-roof hut where a local man warmed himself by a small fire. As we sat together in the quiet of the night, I looked up at the sky. The stars shone with unparalleled brilliance, more vivid than any I'd ever seen, their sheer number piercing the darkness. The serene companionship, the primitive yet beautiful setting, and the vast African sky contributed to a growing sense of peace, hinting at the magical experiences ahead in this remote village.

Despite the intense introduction to Zambia, I was grateful to be away from America. This moment under the African stars, far from the challenges back home, reaffirmed my decision to embark on this journey, promising a profound new chapter. In that moment, with smoke curling into the star-studded sky and my luggage beside the hut, I knew I was on the brink of an epic adventure. Despite the initial hardships, the promise of new discoveries in Central Africa held a compelling allure. I was ready to embrace whatever this journey had in store, armed with newfound resilience and a deep appreciation for the profound moments of connection that marked my arrival. As I settled into the quiet of the night, surrounded by the vast African landscape and the intimate glow of the fire, I sensed the unfolding of a story that would test and transform me. I was in for one hell of a ride.

The first day in Zambia was nothing short of chaos, and I couldn't help but wonder if I had ventured too deep into Africa. But being the adventurous person I was, I couldn't wait to see what this place had in store. As I sat in a small hut in Rufunsa, gazing up at the millions of stars that seemed almost within reach, I knew this adventure would be nothing short of magical.

Starting in the bush.

Awakened by the crowing of roosters right at my doorstep—a sound I had only heard in cartoons—I began my morning in Rufunsa Village. This was a rustic but pleasant surprise. Workers from the nearby hut apartments brought me cereal for breakfast. As I ate, a teenage boy named Elias introduced himself. He was Mwanza's brother and informed me that Mwanza was busy working in the fields but would join us later.

As the morning progressed, Mwanza arrived, and we walked to her house where I met her sister, Jane. Mwanza, Elias, and Jane quickly became central to my experience here. Life in Rufunsa was dramatically different from the village life I had known in Ghana; while that village was only an hour from urban areas, Rufunsa lay deep in the bush—a local term for undeveloped areas.

The family helped secure a room for me on a local man's farm, which was a small hut. This marked the beginning of a true test of my adaptability. The hut lacked a kitchen, bathroom, or water system; my toilet was a hole in the ground, and for toilet paper, I had to collect leaves from trees—a task fraught with caution due to the unseen green mambas lurking among the branches and the ants and scorpions congregating near the hole, adding hazards to this basic necessity. Cooking involved lighting a fire and broiling food over charcoal on the ground, while fetching water required a walk to the well. This was more primitive than I had anticipated, but facing such a raw and challenging lifestyle was thrilling.

During this time, I formed a friendship with Jimmy, the farmkeeper—an older man in his late 40s and an expert in African bush life.

He educated me about the area's dangers, equipped me with a slingshot, and we practiced our aim together. His lessons also covered bush navigation, preparing me for potential encounters with wild animals—a daunting thought his brave demeanor helped ease. Jimmy introduced me to local villagers and taught me phrases in Yanga and Bemba, the predominant languages, helping me integrate and blend in. He even taught me to brew local beer, a common practice here. Watching a woman prepare a 50-gallon jug with pounds of sugar and various ingredients showcased the innovation and creativity of local practices.

One day, I witnessed the slaughter of a large cow—initially shocking, it evolved into a communal gathering that illuminated the necessities of village life. Evenings were dedicated to mastering the art of fire-starting, with Mwanza often dropping by to assist until I finally got the hang of it. Without television to distract me, my nights were filled with reading and, when that grew monotonous, playing Pacman —so much that I nearly reached level 200.

My time in Rufunsa was not merely a survival challenge; it became a period of deep reflection, enabling me to clarify what I truly sought from my journey in Africa. Each day brought new adventures, while each night offered moments to ponder beneath a sky ablaze with stars, the crackling fire my only companion. This experience promised to be the profound adventure I had longed for, immersing me fully in the rhythms of a life so radically different from anything I had ever known.

Slithering, Charging, and Flying Terrors

After a month immersed in the rugged lifestyle of Rufunsa Village, I underwent a profound transformation. Swapping my usual footwear for sandals allowed my feet to breathe in the harsh environment. My aim with the slingshot became nearly flawless, and I mastered the lay of the land, navigating the village pathways like a local. Yet, despite my adaptations, village life remained full of surprises, its raw essence continually challenging me.

One vivid incident showcasing the unpredictability of this life occurred on an ordinary day as I headed back to my hut. The afternoon air was thick when I heard unsettling grunts nearby. I spotted a large bull in the distance, aggressively pawing the ground, its intense gaze locked on me. The air tightened as the bull, in a sudden burst of fury, charged. My instincts kicked in, and I sprinted, barely evading the enraged animal. My heart raced with adrenaline, a reminder of the constant vigilance required here.

Encounters with wild animals were frequent and nerve-wracking. Poisonous cobras slithered across village paths and into the tall grasslands, their presence a constant threat. Most feared was the black mamba, whose lethal venom claimed a chicken outside my room, a grim reminder of lurking dangers. Jimmy and I often found these unfortunate victims during our walks, each discovery heightening the sense of danger in the air.

Yet, nothing prepared me for the sheer terror of a tranquil afternoon turning into a scene from a nightmare.

While Jimmy, his wife, and I chatted beside a hut in an open field, a strange vibration pulsed through the ground, accompanied by a soft but growing buzz. Horror set in as Jimmy identified the source: a massive swarm of over 100,000 Africanized honey bees descending upon us. My blood ran cold at the sight of the dark, swirling mass approaching like a storm.

Thinking quickly, Jimmy pulled me under the hut, his voice calm but firm as he instructed us to remain still. We crouched as the deafening buzz enveloped us, each second stretching into eternity. After what felt like an eternity, the noise began to diminish, and as I cautiously peeked out, I saw the dark cloud of bees drifting away.

Jimmy's voice broke the tense silence, "We're safe now; they're migrating," his words a small comfort after such an ordeal. Emerging from beneath the hut, shaken but unharmed, I questioned the wisdom of venturing into such a remote part of Africa. Despite the fear and close brushes with danger, the thrill of survival and the land's raw beauty compelled me to remain.

Each day presented new challenges, alongside breathtaking beauty and a deep connection to the earth that was both humbling and exhilarating. This was the wild heart of Africa—untamed, unpredictable, and utterly unforgettable.

A White Women's Promise

The most chilling episode of my stay unfolded when Jimmy, a repository of local lore and clandestine tales, approached me with an intriguing proposition. "Do you want to see something interesting?" he asked. Curious, I agreed, and we walked deeper into the village. Our path led us to an astonishing sight: a vast crater, about 40 meters wide, oddly out of place among the dense vegetation.

Standing at the edge, I asked, bewildered, "What is this?" Jimmy, with a tone laced with disdain and resignation, began to recount a tale that sounded almost like a legend. A white woman from the U.S. had once come to the village, professing her intention to create a fishery to aid the local economy. Her proposal won her the trust of the village chief and headman. However, her true motive was far more sinister. Under the guise of constructing the fishery, she had excavated the land, not for fish, but for gold and other minerals. Once she had extracted what she needed, she vanished, leaving behind a gaping hole and a community stripped of its resources, their hopes for prosperity buried beneath the gaping pit.

Jimmy guided me down into the crater, where evidence of exploitation lingered. Glittering traces of gold and colored quartz veins adorned the pit's walls—a vivid reminder of what had been lost. We didn't linger long, though. Jimmy's eyes narrowed as he spotted a group of unfamiliar men approaching, their interest in the pit evident. He whispered urgently, "The mineral trade here is as treacherous as the drug trade in America." His words hastened our departure, but not before I discreetly pocketed a few small stones, tokens of the encounter.

As we retreated from the crater, the implications of Jimmy's words weighed heavily on me. The village still bore signs proclaiming the upcoming fishery—vivid reminders of the deceit that had betrayed their trust. This incident highlighted a hidden truth: even those perceived as benevolent, like the white woman from the United States, could harbor intentions as dark as those of the most notorious criminals.

This realization was further compounded by my discoveries of various colorful gems scattered around the village. To many locals, these were just pretty stones, part of the everyday landscape, their true value unnoticed.

Yet, those in the know—often individuals operating on the fringes of legality—exploited these resources, selling them to foreign buyers from white, Arab, and Chinese backgrounds. This underbelly of the village, intertwined with global demand for its hidden riches, painted a complex picture of exploitation and survival, where the line between right and wrong blurred like the dusty paths crisscrossing the landscape.

As the swarm closed in on the small hut, I felt certain death awaited. The sight of 100,000 killer bees darkening the sky chilled me to the bone. Their furious buzz roared like a chainsaw slicing through the air, intensifying with every heartbeat. The deadly mass surged toward me with terrifying speed, leaving no room for escape.

Using the restroom had turned into an intense ordeal. Leaves served as my only toilet paper, and each time I reached for them, the fear of a lurking green mamba biting me gripped my heart. This risk was part of the territory, and with every movement, I couldn't help but question whether this pursuit of Pan-Africanism would truly be worth it. The stakes were high, yet my hope for something greater remained unwavering.

The white woman's promise to build a fish farm in Rufunsa didn't just leave a gaping hole in the ground; it left a profound emptiness in the hearts of the villagers. Signs still hung, declaring that a fish farm was "coming soon," while some villagers clung to the hope of her return. As I looked around, I couldn't help but wonder what companies she had established with the stolen gold, and what Black Americans back home she might be telling to "pull themselves up by their bootstraps." The void she left behind was more than physical; it was a deep betrayal.

Transitioning to Lusaka from Village Life

After spending considerable time in the rustic village, the novelty of its primitive lifestyle began to fade. The daily routine of bucket showers and leaves for toilet paper was wearing on me. I longed for modern conveniences, a desire that grew stronger with each day. During a visit to a small clothing shop off the highway run by Mwanza and Jane, I shared my restlessness. Both women, whose beauty and spirited conversations I enjoyed, sensed my need for change.

"Mwanza, I'm becoming restless," I confessed after a quiet moment. Her response was both understanding and decisive: "I think it's time for you to relocate to Lusaka, Zambia's largest city." Taking their advice to heart, I packed my bags, bid farewell to Jimmy, and prepared for the next chapter.

The journey to Lusaka was as challenging as any I'd faced in Zambia. The bus was overcrowded, with drivers frequently stopping to cram in more passengers, significantly extending the travel time. By the time we arrived, it was nightfall, adding another layer of complications to finding accommodation.

After an exhausting search, with options dwindling and fatigue setting in, we found a schoolhouse primarily occupied by women. To secure a night's stay, I claimed to be a student from Zimbabwe, a fib that helped reduce potential discrimination. They welcomed me in, and to my relief, the space included both a bathroom and a shower.

As Jane and Mwanza returned to the village, I settled into my new room, feeling a blend of excitement and relief. This transition signified the start of a new phase in Lusaka, providing the modern amenities I had longed for. Here, I was prepared to embrace city life, explore the vibrant urban culture, and establish a routine far removed from the simple yet arduous bush life. This was more than a change of location; it was a fresh start in the true heart of Zambia, brimming with the promise of new adventures and opportunities.

Finding My Groove In Kalingaga

Settling into the bustling life of Lusaka felt like a breath of fresh air after my rugged village experience. Now comfortably housed in the boarding house, life was significantly easier, except for the cold showers. The house, owned by an elderly, affluent Zambian couple, served as a hub of academic activity, which initially suited me as I spent my days exploring the local area and nights crafting music on my computer in the quiet study room.

A friendship developed with a young security guard who lived on the premises. Evenings were filled with discussions about Zambia's economy and local life. One night, he introduced me to a surprising aspect of Lusaka—a well-kept local brothel that revealed the city's economic disparities. This experience illuminated the various ways money circulated in the city, reminiscent of what I had observed in South Africa.

However, life at the boarding house grew repetitive, and the owners began questioning my reasons for staying and my heritage, wondering if I was truly from Africa and what I was doing there. Their suspicion made me realize I needed a change of scenery. Taking it as a sign, I decided to leave, moving to Kalingalinga, a nearby shanty town brimming with life and closer to the city's pulse.

I found accommodation in a student house filled with vibrant, academically driven residents near the University of Zambia. In this new environment, I quickly established a routine: joining a nearby gym, buying a bike for transportation, and engaging with the local community. As the first Black American many locals had encountered, I received a warm welcome. Their curiosity about my background and friendly nature made it easy to forge new friendships, particularly through shared interests like music.

Despite Kalingalinga's reputation for poverty, it provided a safer environment than some of the harsher neighborhoods I had encountered in Johannesburg. Living there deepened my understanding of Zambia's political and economic landscape, particularly the critical role of copper in the region's economy.

Shanty Entrpenuership,

This new chapter in Lusaka allowed me to immerse myself in urban Zambian life and integrate into a vibrant, diverse community. For the first time, I experienced life in an African shanty town, quickly becoming attuned to the rhythm of its lively streets. Local entrepreneurs thrived despite tough conditions, with everything from printing shops and shoe stores to small businesses offering Wi-Fi, herbalists, and makeshift clinics. One local supplier even provided the latest movies, sometimes before they officially hit theaters. The community's creativity and resourcefulness were evident everywhere, with people carving out niches to sustain their livelihoods despite adversity.

However, my immersion came with struggles. An attempt to cook Nshima, Zambia's staple food, went wrong, leaving me bedridden for a week with a severe stomach ailment. Fortunately, a nearby clinic helped me recover quickly, highlighting the importance of building strong connections with local health professionals to navigate the harsher realities of life here.

Street food, while tempting, always felt like a gamble. The stalls, often swarmed by flies, posed a constant risk of cholera and other foodborne illnesses.

The infrastructure in Kalingalinga was challenging. While the main roads were paved, the rest were dust-covered dirt paths, making it hard to keep clean. On rainy days, the streets turned to thick mud, making navigation treacherous. The constant roar of buses, with drivers calling out for passengers until their seats were filled, added to the chaos. Yet, despite the disorder, there was warmth in how they operated—drivers patiently waited for passengers and helped with bags in ways I rarely saw back in the States.

Navigating local transport provided valuable lessons. I was frequently overcharged until friendly locals gave me tips on avoiding common scams, helping me blend in more seamlessly.

Despite these daily challenges, life in Kalingalinga was far more engaging than my earlier experiences in Ghana. While lively and captivating, it lacked the sense of Black unity and Pan-African identity I felt in South Africa. What it lacked in unity, it compensated with a sense of safety and ease. The streets didn't carry the tension I had felt in South Africa, allowing me to move freely without always looking over my shoulder. Despite the challenges, I felt more comfortable and less pressured.

This blend of challenge and charm, hardship and camaraderie, made Kalingalinga a vibrant reflection of urban African life. Amid the dust and energy, I discovered a dynamic community crafting its own narrative in a world many might perceive as daunting. What began as an adventure swiftly evolved into a profound journey, unveiling the essence of urban life in Africa and deepening my understanding of what it means to thrive in unexpected places.

Land Surveying, First Purchase,

After a year of traversing Zambia, my journey shifted from mere observation to establishing a permanent foothold—a place I could truly call home. The time for exploration had passed; now it was time to lay a foundation, testing my resilience and Africa's openness to diasporic connections. With the favorable exchange rate of one U.S. dollar to 17 Zambian Kwacha, my determination to secure land and build a life here solidified.

During this pivotal time, Mwanza, still in the village, informed me of available land. Seizing the opportunity, I boarded a bus to survey the property. Deep in the bush, not far from where I had once stayed near Jimmy's place, lay three acres of fertile land on a mountainside. The area boasted over 100 exotic mango trees, and the ground revealed white marble and rare red aloe vera plants. The land's appeal intensified with the discovery of precious minerals washed down from the mountain during the rainy season. Jimmy, an expert in mineral exploration, would be an invaluable asset in this venture.

The decision to purchase was immediate. The process was surprisingly straightforward: I met with the landowners and the village headman, who facilitated the paperwork. For a modest fee of $1,300, the land was mine. Owning a piece of Africa had become a reality.

However, purchasing the land was only the beginning. The real work lay ahead. Mwanza's grandfather, Mr. Banda, a skilled master builder, agreed to help me bring my vision to life. Together, we drafted blueprints for my new home. Mr. Banda provided a comprehensive list of materials, laying the groundwork for the next phase of construction.

Transportation posed another hurdle. To ensure reliability, I enlisted Angel, a reputable driver in Kalingalinga. In his 40s, Angel had a wealth of knowledge about Zambian life and a reputation for honesty—qualities essential for navigating the challenges of building in a remote area. His experience proved invaluable, particularly in avoiding potential scams.

Now fully immersed in planning and construction, my time in Zambia shifted from exploration to tangible work. Each step brought excitement and challenge as I worked to build not just a house, but a future. This chapter of my journey wasn't merely about laying bricks; it was about creating a lasting legacy and turning dreams into reality in the heart of Africa.

Construction, Negotiation, Adaptation, Corruption, Resilience

Embarking on my first major construction project was both exhilarating and daunting. Mr. Banda and I ventured to a local construction supply store, gathering essential materials—timber, electrical wire, roofing supplies, and over a ton of cement. It was a crash course in survival skills, seeing firsthand the many components needed to build a home from scratch.

We transported everything to my land in Refunsa, where Mr. Banda and his team began marking out the foundation on my three-acre plot. Thankfully, the roadside location made delivery easier, and I quickly saw the value of such a prime spot.

As the foundation took shape, I focused on purchasing 10,000 bricks. The Turkish-owned brick shops dominated the market and offered fair prices, simplifying the transaction process. Coordinating the delivery of bricks, ensuring multiple trucks arrived on time, and verifying the absence of scams was exhausting and required constant vigilance.

Angel proved invaluable during this phase, aiding in negotiations and ensuring fair prices. However, his awareness of my resources made me cautious, reminding me to stay alert even around trusted allies.

As construction progressed, I sought to strengthen my footing in Zambia by acquiring a citizen's card. The process was as slow and corrupt as I had been warned, with long lines outside government offices and officials more focused on their phones than serving the public. With Angel's help, a few "gifts" facilitated the process, revealing the reality of Zambian bureaucracy—money talks. Witnessing officials exploit their own people so blatantly was eye-opening. It was clear that if they treated their own this way, I wouldn't stand a chance as a Black American.

Obtaining my citizen's card marked a significant milestone. It enabled me to open a bank account, and I promptly scheduled an appointment at the DMV. Driving in Zambia posed another challenge —navigating the left-hand side of the road, often without sidewalks, was nerve-wracking, especially after witnessing a deadly accident that heightened my caution. Passing my driving test was a significant relief.

Despite the obstacles, I was making tangible progress. The house was taking shape, my legal status in Zambia was secure, and I was integrating into the local economy. Life here felt raw, yet unlike in America, the opportunities seemed limitless, directly tied to my initiative.

Child's Words Reveal Hidden Truths

The house was nearing completion, with only the roof remaining. I had given Mr. Banda specific instructions, but he opted for a more expensive method, which I suspected was a tactic to inflate labor costs. As expenses spiraled into the thousands, my suspicions grew, culminating in a confrontation. Mr. Banda denied any wrongdoing, but trust between us began to erode.

The cracks in our relationship became more evident one evening when I visited the house to check on progress and spend time with Mwanza and her family. While sitting on the front steps, a young child, no older than five, suddenly dashed out, attempting to snatch my bag while shouting, "Give me the money; you're rich!" This incident spoke volumes, hinting at the private conversations that had likely occurred within the family about me.

Fueled by this incident, I confronted Mwanza, accusing her family of seeing me as a mere source of wealth. Her teenage brother frequently called, asking for a phone or a PlayStation, emphasizing how the family viewed me as a walking ATM rather than a friend or equal partner. I made the decisive choice to dismiss Mr. Banda from the project, creating a deep rift with his family and further straining our ties. The fallout was immediate and bitter. Once warm relationships turned cold, leaving me isolated in a place where I had hoped to build a home and connections.

However, this confrontation toughened me, solidifying my resolve against the corruption woven into daily life. I hired a new contractor to complete the roof, severing ties with Mr. Banda and his network. The house, completed under a new team, stood as a bittersweet reminder of my time in Zambia—beautiful but marked by broken relationships.

Reflecting on the shift from friends to adversaries, I confronted the harsh reality of fleeting friendships in Africa. The phrase "friends come and go" took on deeper meaning, highlighting how corruption could shape and destroy relationships. What began as a vision for a sanctuary transformed into a strategic hub for transporting exotic fruits from my land. It also served as a reminder of the hidden costs of doing business in an environment rife with exploitation.

This chapter of my journey presented a steep learning curve. It revealed not only the challenges of construction but also the fragile nature of trust in a place where relationships could change rapidly. Going forward, I knew I had to be more cautious, ever mindful of the changing dynamics around me.

They say not to discuss sensitive topics in front of children because they tend to repeat them, but in this case, I was grateful for it. It revealed the true nature of the family I was working with, exposing things I wouldn't have known otherwise.

Quick Reflection

Revealing Words: Broken Ties and New Paths

The moment with the child wasn't just surprising; it was a gut punch that shattered my trust. When the young boy violently grabbed my bag, declaring I was rich, it exposed everything. My wealth, rather than my identity, had become the focus of Mwanza's family conversations. The invasion of privacy and open discussions about my money felt like a slap in the face. It confirmed the suspicions I had ignored about Mr. Banda's costly decisions; it was part of a larger manipulation involving the whole family.

What began as unease solidified into cold certainty: this wasn't an accident—it was calculated, and I was being used. What cut deepest was my history with Mwanza. We had known each other since our time in South Africa. She understood my journey as a Black man from America—the struggles, sacrifices, and grind to build a life in Africa. She knew how much this meant to me, making the betrayal feel deeply personal. This was more than money. It was a betrayal of trust, friendship, and the bond we had built.

The situation left me angry and disillusioned. It was a harsh reminder of how quickly relationships can crumble under greed and a brutal lesson about the true cost of pursuing a dream across continents.

Africa's Greatest Resource

After navigating the intricacies of construction and strained friendships, I decided to take a breather and immerse myself back to local life of Lusaka. With my house now complete, I shifted my focus to regular workouts at a well-appointed local gym that boasted a steam room and attracted a friendly crowd of middle to upper-class Zambians. Post-workout, I indulged in street food like cassava, sweet potatoes, and sausages, savoring the flavors of my new environment.

My apartment soon became a hub of intellectual energy, shared with driven students whose dedication to their studies impressed me. Among them was Chileshe, a human calculator whose knack for solving complex mathematical problems became the highlight of our friendly competitions. No matter how tough the equations we threw at her, she always found the answer. Her sharp mind, along with the aspirations of future scientists and financiers around me, revealed the immense potential hidden within Lusaka's youth.

As I explored more of Lusaka, I encountered skilled individuals —true diamonds in the rough—whose potential was often stifled by systemic failures. One enlightening conversation with a friend adept in aquaculture gave me insight into the entrepreneurial spirit thriving beneath the surface. He walked me through the intricacies of fish farming, showing the innovation and resourcefulness just waiting to be unleashed. However, this also revealed a grim reality: outdated cultural norms, coupled with the covert collusion between local governments and white foreign powers, were actively suffocating progress and holding the community back from real advancement.

This stagnation was compounded by the migration of the brightest minds to Europe and the United States, a vivid illustration of the African brain drain—a phenomenon I had only read about but was now witnessing up close. The resignation among locals, watching their best and brightest leave, added a deeper layer to the challenge. Seeing so much untapped potential thwarted by both internal stagnation and external manipulation drove home the sobering reality: without systemic change, the cycle of lost opportunities and unfulfilled potential would continue.

My days became a blend of personal growth and deep reflection on the broader socio-economic challenges confronting this vibrant community. As I settled into the rhythms of everyday life, I was constantly reminded of the resilience and untapped potential of its people. Walking the streets, it became clear that Africa's true wealth wasn't buried in its gold or diamonds but living and breathing around me. The dreams and talents of the people I encountered were more valuable than any mineral wealth, and this realization reshaped my understanding of the true riches of Africa.

Educational Differences

Reflecting on my experiences in both Africa and the United States, I've observed a significant difference in educational environments that deeply affect student outcomes. In Africa, the educational system is robust and highly competitive, with students eager to learn and filled with confidence in their potential. This optimism is largely due to the presence of Black African teachers who can relate directly to their students, fostering a supportive and affirming learning environment free from the negative stereotypes that undermine educational systems in America.

In the U.S., Black American students constantly face systemic discouragement, subtly enforced by a predominance of white teachers. These educators, often carrying unconscious biases, send mixed messages—pointing out students' perceived underachievement while simultaneously highlighting their supposed "advantages," including the claim that being born in America gives them an edge over others. This narrative implies that there is no excuse for their struggles, framing academic difficulties as personal failings while ignoring the systemic barriers these students face..

The disparity becomes even clearer when considering African students who migrate to the U.S. Many of these students, often older and from higher socio-economic backgrounds, including some from royal families, have had access to better educational opportunities before migrating. This skews comparisons against Black American students, who must navigate a far more challenging educational landscape filled with systemic obstacles.

I recall my own school days in the U.S., where students from war-torn Darfur were often used as examples to undermine the efforts of Black American students. Teachers would say, "They come from a war zone and still succeed—what's your excuse?" This kind of scrutiny only added to the already heavy burdens placed on Black American youth.

Despite the achievements of some African students, it's important to recognize that the majority of Africa's population—up to 80%—still lives in poverty. Those who receive an education represent only the top 3-7%, many of whom aspire to leave for the U.S. or Europe after completing their studies. This contrasts with Black Americans, who, despite facing significant hardships, rarely consider mass migration as a solution.

The sense of safety and community trust in Africa, where children can hitchhike to school without fear, is completely different from the dangerous environments Black American students navigate. In Africa, I saw children as young as four walking the streets or catching rides to school with strangers, unafraid and untouched by gang violence, police brutality, or visible drug activity. The difference is undeniable. In the U.S., Black American students face these threats daily, adding layers of stress before they even reach their classrooms.

Seeing the safe and supportive educational environment in Africa, where students are uplifted and encouraged, only emphasizes the grave injustices faced by Black Americans. This deepened my understanding of the systemic challenges Black Americans endure, revealing a situation even more dire than I had previously comprehended.

Community/ Health

In Zambia, the strength of family bonds and communal connections ensures that very few people are left homeless, even though poverty is widespread. Families and community members step in, offering places to stay and support during hard times. This communal safety net creates a system where, despite financial hardship, people rarely face destitution alone. In America, by contrast, people often face their struggles in isolation, with far less support from extended family or neighbors. There, homelessness is a glaring issue, where individuals are more likely to be left to fend for themselves.

Despite these strong family ties, many Zambians of all ages wander the streets in search of sporadic work. This shows a complex reality: a society rich in social bonds but lacking in opportunities. Even with this challenge, people remain connected through family and community, creating a safety net that's nearly absent in the urban life of America.

On the health front, Zambia presents a mixed picture. Obesity is uncommon, thanks to diets rich in home-grown, chemical-free foods and a lifestyle that involves frequent walking. However, this benefit is offset by a low life expectancy, revealing serious gaps in healthcare that contradict the visible vitality of the people.

The relentless 9-to-5 grind that dominates American life, with its constant pressure of living paycheck to paycheck, is far less common in Zambia. Life moves at a more relaxed pace, supported by strong community ties, which makes the quality of life feel more humane and less stressful than the high-pressure environments Americans consider normal. From what I observed, Africans seem to enjoy better mental health, as they aren't burdened by the same levels of mental stress that many Americans endure. The communal support and slower pace of life offer a natural buffer against the anxieties and pressures that often define life in the West.

Yet, the idea of America as a land of endless wealth and opportunity is often romanticized in Zambia, ignoring the harsh realities of poverty and struggle faced by many. There's a widespread belief that everyone in America is rich, with some even genuinely believing that money grows on trees. This disconnect shows how Western life is idealized without a true understanding of the deep social and economic challenges it holds.

This reflection raises an important question: what truly defines a 'better' quality of life? It challenges the notion that the materialistic American lifestyle surpasses the communal, supportive way of life found in places like Zambia. Here, strong community bonds form a vital safety net—one sorely lacking in the West—pushing us to reconsider whether material wealth alone guarantees a richer, more fulfilling life.

The striking difference between African schools and what Black Americans endure was glaring. African students are taught by African teachers who understand them fully and are invested in their future, preparing them to lead their countries. However, in America, white teachers work hand–in–hand with the police systems, channeling Black children toward prison instead of toward opportunity. The distinction couldn't be more profound.

For The Love of Trump

One of the most eye-opening realities I encountered in Lusaka was the deep political frustration simmering among the people. Nearly everyone I spoke to carried a heavy sense of betrayal, accusing their African leaders of cowardice and abandonment. These leaders, they said, were more focused on appeasing foreign powers—whether Chinese, European, or otherwise—than on uplifting their own citizens. The resentment ran deep, but what struck me most was an unexpected sentiment that surfaced in conversation after conversation: many Africans openly wished for a president like Donald Trump.

They admired his unapologetic strength, his refusal to bend to outside pressures, and his ability to make bold, uncompromising decisions. In Zambia—and in other African nations I traveled to—Trump wasn't just respected, he was revered in ways that caught me off guard.

This revelation forced me to take a hard look at the situation in Black America. For far too long, we've been handed leaders who serve the same white-dominated system, offering us little more than symbolic gestures while perpetuating the same cycle of oppression. What we need is the same thing many Africans longed for: a leader with the audacity to stand firm, someone unafraid to demand what is rightfully ours. Not another puppet of the system, but a true champion for the people—someone with the same boldness that made Trump an unlikely figure of admiration across parts of Africa.

This unexpected observation left me rethinking the very essence of leadership. What does true leadership look like? Not just for Africa, but for Black Americans too. It wasn't about agreeing with Trump's policies; it was about recognizing the qualities of strength and conviction that, in desperate times, make people look to someone who refuses to play by the rules of a broken system. And maybe, just maybe, that's exactly what we need.

The True African Americans

There was a fascinating moment worth reflecting on about my friend Rose, a charming, sophisticated Zambian-American from New England who, like me, wanted to build a life in Zambia. We met at a restaurant near downtown Lusaka, and quickly became friends, sharing the same aspirations of reconnecting with Africa. But what stood out to me the most was her unique perspective—born in Zambia but raised in America, her challenges were even more complex than mine because she had family here, and their treatment of her was rooted in exploitation.

Because she was born in America, her Zambian relatives constantly expected her or her parents to solve their financial problems. She was no longer seen as a Zambian but as a "Zambian-American"—an outsider in her own country. Her family didn't welcome her as kin returning home; they saw her as a potential benefactor whose success in America they felt entitled to.

Rose's story exposed a broader issue that many Africans face when returning to their home countries after living abroad. Many don't return because of jealous family members who never had the opportunity to migrate. Others, like Rose, have outgrown the cultural norms still practiced in Africa, creating a disconnect between who they've become and their family's expectations. Adding to this, the threat of black magic and curses from envious relatives adds another layer of complexity. Once an African moves abroad, they are no longer just "African." They straddle two worlds, often struggling to fully belong in either. Rose's experience helped me understand why many Africans in the diaspora distance themselves from their ancestral homelands.

This reality sheds light on why many in the diaspora distance themselves from their ancestral homelands. They navigate family pressures, financial expectations, and the risk of being targeted for scams. Their time away changes them, and upon returning, they often find themselves viewed as foreigners, caught between two worlds and never fully belonging.

This observation made me distance myself even further from the term "African-American." Unlike African migrants, Black Americans don't have a specific country to "return" to in Africa. We don't share the same family ties or cultural expectations. Our experiences on the continent are fundamentally different. And it reaffirmed a truth I had been grappling with—Black Americans are truly American, more than anyone else, because they are foundational to the United States, not immigrants to it. For all the injustices we face there, it's still our home.

As Rose's frustrations grew, she eventually made the choice to return to America, where the challenges—though real—were familiar. She explained that she'd rather face the racism from white Americans than endure the mistreatment she was experiencing in Africa. Her final words before departure were chilling: "I'd rather be seen as a nigger in America than live here as an African.

I must add, no matter how many flags an African living in America waves or how many cultural symbols they display on social media, their biggest fear is being sent back to their home countries. Despite their vocal pride, exaggerated accents, and claims of having a deeper connection to their culture, much of it is a facade. They know the harsh realities of life back home, and the truth is, many are desperate to avoid returning. This outward display of cultural pride often hides a deeper struggle with identity—one that they project onto Black Americans in an attempt to assert some sense of superiority. They present themselves as having a closer connection to their roots, but back home, many Africans still feel like outsiders, dealing with their own internal crisis.

We Work Hard Myth

The idea that Africans arrive in America with nothing is a myth. From what I've observed during my time in Africa, many who migrate to the U.S. or Europe come from well-off families or have strong connections—whether through government officials, white missionaries, or other influential sponsors. While they often claim to have struggled to reach the U.S., the reality is that many had financial advantages back home. For those unfamiliar with Africa, these surface-level stories of hardship rarely reveal the full complexity of their circumstances.

The frequent comparison between African migrants and Black Americans is not only misleading but also perpetuates harmful stereotypes. African immigrants are often portrayed as more hardworking or successful, yet, many of these migrants come from the top 0.5% of their home countries, benefiting from resources and privileges that most of their fellow citizens don't have.

These migrants often come from elite families or receive financial backing, granting them significant advantages before they even set foot in the U.S. Meanwhile, Black Americans—who are often labeled as lazy—have overcome generations of systemic oppression, including slavery, segregation, and mass incarceration, while achieving high-level positions across various fields long before these migrants arrived. This raises a critical question: If African migrants are so capable, why aren't they fixing the systemic problems in their own countries?

One moment that made this clear to me was witnessing how whites in Africa vet Africans for potential migration to the U.S. I saw this firsthand during a meeting at East Park Mall in Lusaka. A friend of mine was being assessed by a white man who had the power to sponsor his migration. I watched as my friend performed exceptionally well [Cooned], earning the approval he needed to secure a path to America. He's there now, benefiting from the opportunities vetted and granted by a gatekeeper, which further reinforces that many African migrants aren't struggling to escape their countries—they're often handpicked for success abroad.

During my time in Africa, I witnessed firsthand how significant the difference in starting points can be. Even a lower-income Black American moving to Africa would likely find themselves in the top 1–4% in terms of wealth and opportunity. They could easily buy land, start businesses, and thrive while locals continue to struggle with basic survival. This disparity in resources highlights how unfair it is to compare the two groups.

From my findings, the wave of African immigration is part of a sophisticated form of white supremacy. It operates as a way to mask the ongoing Black genocide against Black Americans by replacing them with a more passive, less resistant Black African and Caribbean population. This immigration shift provides a more favorable and compliant group while continuing to overlook the systemic issues facing Black Americans. While African migrants bring talent and ambition, their presence is being used to undermine the Black American struggle for justice and equality, presenting a dangerous distraction from the real issues at play.

Tribalism

Another aspect I came to understand was how deeply rooted tribalism is across the African continent. In every African country, there are dozens of tribes, each with its own hierarchy. Typically, one tribe is seen as superior while others are regarded as less significant. In Nigeria, the Hausa tribe is viewed as the dominant one, while the Fulani are considered lower. In Zambia, the Bembas hold the top spot, but the Tongas are often the most despised.

Tribal loyalty runs so deep that during national elections, Africans will only vote for candidates from their own tribe, often rejecting others regardless of their qualifications. This practice, born from centuries of allegiance, ensures that political divides often mirror ethnic ones, making it nearly impossible for nations to unify under a single leadership. When Africans migrate to the U.S., these tribal conflicts and prejudices don't just vanish—they tag along, dictating how African immigrants interact with each other and with Black Americans.

In the U.S., Black Americans are regarded as the most influential and culturally dominant Black community globally. However, African immigrants, many of whom come from tribes with long-standing rivalries, view Black Americans not as part of a larger Black family, but as another "tribe"—one that now overshadows them. This shift in status can breed envy, especially since many African immigrants hail from what are considered the "superior" tribes in their own countries. Accustomed to tribal dominance back home, they now find themselves living in Black America's cultural shadow, which can stir resentment.

Most Black Americans are unaware of the tribal conflicts that shape African societies, and without this context, they may not understand the source of this tension. African immigrants often bring their rivalries with them, projecting these historical animosities onto Black Americans. What might seem like cultural friction is often rooted in deeper, ancient divisions, which can manifest as subtle or even overt hostility.

What disturbed me most was realizing that white supremacists had studied these divisions and weaponized them against Black Americans. The tribal conflicts that foster resentment among Africans could easily be transplanted to America, fueling tension rather than unity. Many Black Americans believed that the arrival of more Black faces would naturally lead to greater solidarity, but they underestimated the impact of these deeply rooted tribal dynamics. This exploitation of division may be one of the most sophisticated strategies used to weaken Black unity, pitting us against each other in ways we often fail to recognize.

These insights gave me a deeper understanding of African migration, internal conflicts, and how these dynamics shape political and social views. They revealed the complex reality of how African migrants adapt to American society and the profound disconnect between the lived experiences of Africans on the continent and Black Americans. This knowledge exposed the underlying factors that obstruct meaningful solidarity across the global Black diaspora. This "anti-Black tribalism" complicates efforts toward Pan-African unity by viewing Black Americans as competitors.

SIDE NOTE

This tribalism among Africans presents a dangerous situation for Black Americans, especially given the growing presence of African immigrants in key roles across the U.S. Many work as doctors in hospitals, serve as police officers and correctional staff, and, more troubling, some even represent Black Americans in political spaces like the Congressional Black Caucus. Additionally, African students are enrolling in large numbers at HBCUs, with events like "Africa Takeover Day" at Howard University—a historically Black college—further demonstrating that African immigrants do not see themselves as part of a unified Black identity with Black Americans.

Africa's Perception of Women/ Men Value

One of the most eye-opening and admirable aspects I observed in Africa was their approach to relationships and the value placed on women. In many communities, when a man wanted to marry a woman, he had to pay lobola—a bride price, typically in the form of money or cows, given to her family to release her into marriage. The price was determined by the woman's qualities. A young woman who was educated, in excellent physical shape, well-mannered, and from a respected family could be worth as much as 40 cows. However, if that same woman had a child out of wedlock, her value would drop dramatically—perhaps to five cows. With two or more children, her value diminished to the point where her family wouldn't ask for anything in exchange. Age also played a significant role—an older woman, regardless of her qualities, would command a much lower price.

This system revealed a notable disparity compared to the dynamics in the United States. In America, women with multiple children often still see themselves as deserving of the highest-value men, believing their worth remains unchanged. However, this perception doesn't align with how society views them, even if it's unspoken. In Africa, the consequences of having children outside of marriage or advancing in age were clear and directly impacted how a woman was valued by her family and potential suitors.

For men, the process was just as demanding, requiring them to present themselves to the woman's family, who would then decide if he was qualified to marry their daughter. Often, the family would also want to meet his parents, assessing the quality of his upbringing. In Africa, upstanding men with stable jobs, entrepreneurs, and business owners were highly sought after—completely different from the U.S., where street culture is often glorified. In America, even highly accomplished Black men with great careers and education are often seen as "lame" or less desirable by many women, while street guys are propped up. But in Africa, these same men were revered by African women and society.

This difference in how value is assessed—both for men and women—was one of the most profound cultural lessons I took from my time there. In Africa, there was a direct correlation between life choices and one's perceived worth, something largely overlooked in the U.S., where societal expectations don't match reality. The white supremacist, feminist-driven culture in America has distorted perceptions of value, particularly among Black Americans. Traditional views on relationships and respect for decent men have eroded, with women frequently drawn to street culture instead of recognizing the value in men who build stable, productive lives.

Equally striking was how "hoe culture" in Africa was harshly condemned. Women who engaged in such behavior were viewed as prostitutes and heavily stigmatized. Even though prostitution is widespread throughout Africa, the women involved were fully aware of their diminished social standing and knew their place within their respective nations. They didn't attempt to elevate their status beyond what was widely understood. In contrast, strip club culture in America has seeped into everyday life within many Black communities, normalizing behaviors that, in Africa, would be seen as degrading. Many women in this culture mistakenly believe they remain high-value despite their actions, as flaunting oneself or acting provocatively for attention isn't just discouraged—it's considered a mark of shame.

This fundamental difference in how promiscuity and self-worth are viewed highlights a deeper cultural divide between Africa and the United States. While Africa maintains clear social boundaries regarding these behaviors, the U.S. has blurred the lines, leading to confusion about value and entitlement, especially among women who don't recognize the broader social consequences of their actions. These perceptions are not just individual choices; they ripple outward, profoundly damaging Black American social scenes, dating dynamics, and ultimately, family structures. The normalization of promiscuity and inflated self-worth has made it harder for genuine relationships to form and flourish. Families, the cornerstone of any community, suffer as these distorted values perpetuate poor decision-making and broken homes, deepening a cycle of instability that is harder to break.

A More Ambitious Project

After securing my first land purchase, I felt rejuvenated and ready to tackle more ambitious projects. Once again partnering with Angel, we searched the outskirts of Lusaka for viable land. City plots were tangled in family disputes and bureaucratic red tape, which complicated the search for clear titles. The chaos of urban life, coupled with corrupt police constantly targeting me for bribes, prompted me to seek refuge beyond the city limits.

Chongwe became my focus—a peaceful town located about 30 minutes from Lusaka, known for its relaxed pace and spacious land parcels. Situated near the airport along the Great East Road, it offered not only tranquility but also a strategic escape route, should I need it. The area had the perfect blend of rural charm and accessibility, with ample building supplies and a friendly community atmosphere.

After weeks of searching, I found the perfect spot: a vast tract of land about the size of two football fields, ideally situated by the roadside near the headman's palace and close to the serene Chongwe River. Learning it was for sale, I seized the opportunity. Disguising my identity as a local to evade inflated prices, Angel and I negotiated with the landowners, and soon, the land was mine—larger and more strategically located than my first plot.

However, this new land, while ideal, was wild and untamed, requiring significant work before any construction could begin. The area was filled with wildlife that seemed straight out of a thriller— venomous black mambas and puff adders, seven-foot-long Nile monitor lizards, and massive spiders. I hired a team to clear the wilderness, preparing the ground for development. Angel recommended a skilled builder, and together we drafted blueprints for what would serve as my main residence—a larger and more ambitious project than any I'd previously undertaken.

As the team worked to carve out a road for truck access and cultivate the land, I could feel the adrenaline of tackling something this big. With the land ready and blueprints in place, I was embarking on a new adventure—one that promised not just a home, but a deeper engagement with the land and community of Chongwe. The stakes were high, but the potential was exhilarating. As the project progressed, it became clear that I wasn't just building a house; I was shaping a future in the heart of Africa, surrounded by its wild beauty and complex challenges.

Taming The Wild Life & Managing Construction

The construction of my new home in Chongwe had truly taken off, becoming a hub of activity that drew the attention of the local community. With 14,000 bricks and essential materials secured, the site buzzed with progress. The influx of villagers seeking employment was overwhelming, and I hired as many as I could, understanding the importance of providing opportunities in this quiet part of Zambia. The sheer number of people eager for work underscored the impact of such development on the area. To manage the growing crowds and preserve privacy, I took the significant step of fencing the entire perimeter of the property, establishing a boundary between the construction zone and the outside world.

The architectural vision for the house was bold and innovative—an open-concept design with two bedrooms to maximize the spaciousness of the living areas. This design wasn't just for aesthetic appeal; it was practical for managing the space efficiently. Anticipating the infrastructural challenges of the region, I incorporated sustainability into the design: solar panels lined the roof to harness the sun, and a borehole connected to a 3,000-gallon water tower ensured a reliable water supply. This setup not only ensured the house was self-sufficient but also established a new standard in the area.

However, the road to completion was fraught with challenges. The rainy season turned the landscape into mud, hindering movement and increasing the risk of encounters with local wildlife. Black mambas posed frequent hazards, prompting me to install concrete pads extending ten meters from the house to deter these creatures. The recent death of a Japanese man, swallowed whole by an African rock python nearby, served as a chilling reminder of the dangers. Along with sightings of camel spiders, tarantulas, and giant centipedes, the need for pest control became urgent.

Managing the construction wasn't just about design and environmental concerns; it required resilience in the face of bureaucratic hurdles and the daily management of a diverse workforce. It became a balancing act of logistics and diplomacy, with trucks delivering materials, workers navigating the intricacies of the build, and constant vigilance against regular scams targeting me.

Despite the challenges—managing the workforce, dealing with government red tape, and mitigating wildlife risks—the project moved forward. Every day brought new lessons in resilience and resourcefulness, deepening my commitment to this land. While the idea of a unified 'Blackness' remained elusive, building a life here on my own terms was a testament to the enduring spirit of adventure and the pursuit of a dream deeply rooted in African soil.

Interested Friends, Reminders of Instability

The land was nearly tamed to its fullest potential, ready for cultivation. Sunflowers, natural herbs, peanuts, and other crops sprouted from the fertile soil, marking a newfound wealth. This abundance began to draw attention from my Black American friends back home, many of whom were grappling with racial issues and intrigued by the potential I had shared.

Motivated by my stories, my friend Chris flew over to see the land for himself. Astonished by what he saw, he was inspired to purchase his own plot. A brief tour around the city and the university cemented his decision to build a life in Zambia. Shortly after Chris left to settle his affairs back home, a sudden eruption of violence highlighted the fortunate timing of his departure.

My decision to build outside Lusaka, in the quieter Chongwe area, was soon validated under alarming circumstances. Riots erupted in the city, with scenes painfully reminiscent of Hotel Rwanda. At night, masked individuals hurled poison gas into communities, stirring panic and chaos among the populace, many of whom suspected government involvement. The city streets transformed into a scene of destruction, cluttered with burned tires and debris, while men armed with machetes targeted anyone within reach.

During one particularly harrowing incident, Angel and I found ourselves trapped as the road was blocked by burning tires. As men wielding machetes and blunt objects tried to pull me from the car, Angel skillfully navigated through the chaos, narrowly escaping the escalating violence.

The situation took an even more dire turn when the military intervened, deploying helicopters and tanks to disperse the crowds. Amidst the chaos, I found myself in the midst of thousands of protesters as the military began firing indiscriminately into the crowd. The air was filled with screams and confusion as bullets flew without regard for human life, striking down several people around me. In a desperate bid for safety, I rushed into a friend's nearby restaurant. We barricaded ourselves inside as the sounds of gunfire and chaos echoed outside. This harrowing experience highlighted the military's brutal response to the civil unrest, leaving me shaken and deeply disturbed by the blatant disregard for human life.

The riots exposed the extreme dangers that can arise suddenly in Africa—often hidden from short-term visitors who experience only fleeting hospitality and tranquility. For residents, the reality is complex; surface peace can quickly give way to deeper, more dangerous forces. As the chaos subsided, I found sanctuary in my home in Chongwe, grateful for its peaceful seclusion. This retreat reaffirmed my decision to build away from the city's unpredictable violence.

During this time, the words of an older village woman resonated deeply. Watching the aimless crowds and mounting chaos, she remarked, "The African people are like flies, busy doing nothing." Her observation cut through the disarray, reflecting a pervasive futility. It was a poignant reminder of Zambia's contradictions—beauty and potential on one hand, instability and unpredictability on the other. Life here was a delicate balance between these extremes, constantly reminding me of the complex nature of my journey.

One Families Trash, Another Persons Treasure

As the smoke cleared, life resumed its normal rhythm, as if chaos had never engulfed the city. Blinded by my commitment to Pan-Africanism, I remained resolute in my determination to press forward. Weeks were spent searching for fruit trees to enrich the land. I acquired four varieties of oranges, lemons, avocado trees, and a diverse array of berry bushes. The crown jewel of my orchard—the elusive dragon fruit—was found on a farm owned by a Zambian minister.

As my orchard took shape, the fertile African soil produced fruit within months. Eating my first homegrown oranges and dragon fruit filled me with a deep sense of accomplishment. It was my first time successfully growing food, and the taste of that hard-earned fruit was a milestone in my journey towards self-sustainability. Yet, just as optimism bloomed, new challenges emerged—more daunting than the wild creatures I had previously encountered.

The previous landowners, who had long abandoned the property, suddenly resurfaced, their eyes filled with envy. Whispers spread throughout the village about my identity as a Black American, fueling growing resentment. What was once a neglected piece of land became a coveted prize as they saw the thriving fruit trees and life I had cultivated.

In search of resolution, I turned to the local headman, hoping to quell the rising hostility. Angel, invaluable in navigating local dynamics, played a key role in defusing tensions. However, his growing dependence on me for daily sustenance weighed heavily, shifting our partnership into a delicate balance of reliance and obligation.

As I navigated these intricate dynamics, a profound truth emerged: what is discarded by some can be cherished by others. This realization struck me as I navigated this treacherous terrain, highlighting the complexity of human desire and ownership in Africa's unpredictable landscape.

Shielded Amidst Global Turmoil

As my farm flourished, transforming the landscape and multiplying my wealth tenfold, I found myself in a powerful and sustainable position. With a growing network and increasing influence, I was well-equipped to counter local schemes aimed at undermining my success or stealing my resources. Recognizing the potential for expansion, I began purchasing more land, both for myself and to broker deals for Black Americans looking to relocate to Africa. Aware of the scam-ridden local real estate market, I sought to simplify the process for newcomers, shielding them from the predatory practices I had once faced.

Amid this period of strategic growth, and before Chris arrived, I purchased a car to enhance my mobility and independence. This enhanced my project management, maintained my privacy, reduced my reliance on Angel, and kept my activities discreet.

However, just as my endeavors were flourishing, a new and unexpected threat emerged. Whispers of COVID-19 began circulating around Zambia, and within weeks, the global pandemic plunged the world into chaos. Initially, Zambia seemed untouched by the virus, and life went on as usual. But soon after, the government swiftly declared a national emergency, enforcing mask mandates with armed guards and locking down daily life despite widespread skepticism.

As the pandemic escalated, Chris found himself stranded in Johannesburg, which quickly transformed into what I heard was a war zone. The crisis worsened social and economic tensions, leading to rampant crime and violence. Tanks rolled through the streets, enforcing strict pandemic regulations with brutal force.

Back in Zambia, my secluded home in Chongwe became a refuge from the global upheaval. The isolation of my property shielded me from the chaos gripping the world. Life in my community remained largely unchanged; the villagers, far removed from government oversight, carried on without masks, seemingly untouched by the pandemic's looming presence.

This period of isolation stretched on for over seven months, during which the outside world appeared to spiral further into crisis. When Chris finally escaped South Africa, the relief was evident. He arrived in Zambia, relieved to leave behind what he called a "failed state," exhausted from the pandemic's chaos.

Although my own time in South Africa had been filled with positive experiences, I, too, had recognized the simmering dangers and hostility just beneath the surface. It was this very undercurrent of instability that had driven me to leave South Africa, seeking a more peaceful and secure future elsewhere. Zambia, with its tranquil and isolated environment, felt like a sanctuary in comparison, further validating my decision to settle here.

Throughout these challenges, my estate became more than just a physical refuge—it was a reminder of the foresight that had secured my stability. While the world outside wrestled with unprecedented chaos, my corner of Zambia remained peaceful and stable, a testament to the value of self-sufficiency and careful planning. As the world struggled with the disruptions of COVID-19, another seismic event shook the globe: the murder of George Floyd, a brutal act that sparked worldwide outrage.

His death ignited protests across the U.S., leading to uprisings worldwide. From London to the Middle East, protesters decried injustice, with some even dubbing it the "beginning of the end of America." Demonstrations erupted from Brazil to Japan, with millions demanding change.

From over 9,000 miles away, I watched as the world rallied for Black rights and systemic reform. Yet, despite this global fervor, the African nations around me remained unnervingly silent. While the rest of the world was engulfed in protest, the local population continued on with little reaction. The streets and homes in Africa stayed calm, revealing a profound disconnect from the outrage unfolding abroad.

Chris had just arrived, and together we watched the news, disturbed by Africa's silence. The indifference was baffling, showcasing the complex social and political dynamics that made the distant unrest seem irrelevant to the people here. The irony was striking: the land often hailed as the "motherland" seemed unmoved by the struggles of their kin abroad.

During this period of global upheaval, news reached me from an inside source about an emergency summit of African leaders in Addis Ababa, Ethiopia. Rumors suggested they were strategizing on how to maintain their silence amid global protests for Black justice. The secrecy surrounding this gathering amidst global calls for change painted a chilling picture of Africa's disconnect from the broader fight for Black liberation.

Watching these events unfold felt surreal, as if I were witnessing two completely different worlds—one on fire with passion and uprising, the other shrouded in unsettling calm. This moment was profound—while a global Black liberation movement raged, Africa remained disturbingly quiet. Even after the protests died down, I couldn't shake one haunting thought: how could Japan, a country with no cultural ties, fight harder for Black lives than the entire continent of Africa?

I amassed significant wealth from this ambitious project, with immediate rewards. Protected from global crises and powered by solar panels and a deep well, the land became an abundant resource. Exotic fruits and herbs flourished in Africa's rich soil, growing with an intensity I had never witnessed. In just months, I rose from a thousandnaire to a millionaire, witnessing my hard work transform into something tangible and powerful. Yet, with that success came a shadow—the weight of envy from those who observed it unfold.

I couldn't help but wonder why the African Union called an emergency meeting during the George Floyd uprisings. The timing felt too significant to be a coincidence. As I watched the world rise up for Black liberation, the blackest continent on earth remained eerily quiet. It struck me then—how could Japan, a nation so far removed from this struggle, make more noise than Africa itself during such a pivotal moment?

Kidnapping and Extortion

The initiation into city life in Lusaka for my friend Chris began smoothly. We navigated the essentials—acquiring his citizen card and driver's license, tasks I had already mastered. Settled comfortably on a quiet street in Kulundu, I was eager to introduce him to the best local spots, from eateries to the city's vibrant nightlife.

However, our relaxed evening took a violent turn during what should have been a casual stroll to a nearby restaurant. Without warning, a truck screeched to a halt beside us, and two military men armed with AK-47s jumped out. These were the night marauders—predators who used the cover of darkness to abduct and extort their victims. Their fearsome reputation preceded them. A friend from Cameroon had once told me about his own harrowing kidnapping at the hands of similar men. These people operated with impunity, and now we were their latest targets. Taken right off the street, we had no time to resist and no chance to escape. They demanded money, assuming from our foreign accents that we were wealthy.

With no cash on me, Chris had to negotiate our release. The tension was suffocating, but their impatience was even more dangerous. They drove us back to our residence, where they held me at gunpoint while Chris rushed inside to gather the ransom. The cold metal of the gun against my skin was a harsh reminder of how quickly life can spiral out of control.

As I sat there, calculating every option, I knew that if the situation escalated, I'd have to fight for my life. In places like this, things rarely end peacefully. My mind flashed to a recent incident in Nigeria, where a white American man had been kidnapped after handing over just $40.

Unsatisfied, they demanded $1 million for his release, stemming from the belief that all Americans are wealthy. His story had a rare ending—Navy SEALs stormed in, killing the kidnappers and rescuing him. But we were Black, and we knew we wouldn't have that kind of rescue. Here, that dangerous belief in American wealth left us exposed. If it came down to it, I was ready to fight rather than become another casualty of this unpredictable land.

The wait for Chris felt endless, each second stretching out as the danger mounted. The kidnappers grew more agitated, their threats sharper and more desperate. I could sense how close they were to losing control, and I knew it wouldn't take much to push them over the edge. Finally, after what felt like an eternity, Chris returned with the ransom. The atmosphere was suffocating, thick with tension as the money changed hands. But then, just as suddenly as they had appeared, the men vanished into the night, leaving behind a silence that echoed with the weight of what had just happened.

That night left a deep scar on both of us. For Chris, the excitement of starting a new life in Zambia had been shattered. For me, it reinforced why I had chosen to distance myself from the dangers of city life. The chaotic unpredictability of Lusaka was a risk I no longer wanted to take, and this ordeal only hastened Chris's decision to relocate to the safety and calm of the countryside.

Despite the horror of the experience, our belief in Pan-Africanism and our desire to escape the racism of our homeland remained unshaken. However, this incident served as a reminder of the volatility simmering beneath the surface in Africa's cities. My decision to build away from the urban sprawl had proven wise, and the peace of my estate became not just a refuge but a sanctuary from the unpredictable violence of Lusaka.

Walking at night in Lusaka required sharp awareness.
Poverty was rampant, and ironically, the police were
some of the biggest thieves. While the city was generally
safe, encounters with military police could quickly turn
dangerous. A routine stop could easily shift from petty
extortion to something far worse, especially once they
heard an American accent—kidnapping was never out of
the question.

Individualism, Parting Ways, New Ventures

We packed Chris's belongings and set off for Chongwe, eager to settle him into a new chapter of our journey. A room at a local hotel, known for its convenient month-to-month payment options, became his introduction to the slower, quieter pace of town life. The area buzzed with friendly locals, and it wasn't long before we met Chanda, who worked at the nearby brick shop, and her brother Paul. This sibling pair quickly became like family, always ready to lend a hand, whether it was for a simple favor or more urgent needs like car troubles. Their kindness and support were invaluable during those early days as Chris adjusted.

Once Chris was comfortably settled, the next major task was securing land for him. I offered him a portion of the land I had already purchased—just 30 seconds down the road from my place—as a way to help ease the transition and avoid the typical pitfalls of land-buying scams.

However, Chris preferred to find his own plot. After some searching, we found a piece of land about 15 minutes from mine, deeper into the village. While I had some concerns about the distance, knowing it might stretch our resources and make us more vulnerable, I understood Chris's desire to create something that was entirely his own. It wasn't that we were on different paths; it was simply a reflection of his need for independence, even though it introduced new challenges.

Securing his land turned into a long and exhausting ordeal, largely due to the headman's hesitation to finalize the deal. While we faced these delays, I shifted my attention to expanding my ventures. I acquired a prime plot along Chailambana Road, close to the University of Chongwe, with plans to transform it into a cultural hub—a movie theater that would serve as a community landmark. Nearby, I also found an apartment with the perfect amenities, positioning me for the next phase of growth.

This period of land acquisition wasn't just about expanding my footprint; it also led to shifts in my relationship with Angel. I had always believed in helping others grow alongside me, so I offered to fund five different business ideas he had, hoping it would encourage him to step into entrepreneurship. However, instead of embracing the opportunity, Angel's dependency on me deepened. He began to expect financial support for his everyday needs, even when there wasn't work to justify it. What started as a partnership began to feel more like a one-sided arrangement.

Despite my hopes for his success, it became clear that this dynamic wasn't sustainable. Eventually, I had to make the tough decision to step back and move forward on my own. It wasn't an easy choice, and it left me with a lingering sense of disappointment, but it was necessary for both of us.

As the theater project progressed, I suggested that Chris move into my home for security and efficiency. We could pool resources, work more closely together, and he could save on rent. True to his independent nature, he declined, preferring to maintain his own space. I respected his decision, but it made me realize we were approaching life here from different perspectives.

In Africa, I'd observed how communities like the Chinese, Indians, and Turks pooled resources, shared land, and built strong networks to navigate the challenges of daily life. Their unity wasn't just cultural—it was a practical strategy for survival, giving them an edge in unpredictable environments. Chris, like many Black Americans, valued independence and self-reliance—traits deeply ingrained in our culture. While these qualities are admirable, particularly in the U.S., where individual success is celebrated, Africa's often hostile and unpredictable environment showed me that collective strength was a necessity. It wasn't just about thriving; sometimes it was about surviving.

The parallels to America were striking. Black Americans, too, face a hostile environment characterized by systemic racism and social inequality. However, similar to Africa, this hostile landscape complicates our ability to unite as a collective. The same individualism that gives us resilience in the face of oppression also weakens our ability to come together as a community. In both contexts, the unpredictability of the environment—whether systemic challenges in the U.S. or on-the-ground dangers in Africa—demands collective effort, yet individualism often hinders our ability to realize our full strength.

Chris's decision to live independently reflected a mindset many of us are raised with, yet highlighted a key difference in approach. In Africa, unity isn't just a cultural value; it's a survival strategy. Pooling resources, relying on trusted networks, and working together is how communities protect themselves in a difficult, unpredictable landscape. In America, systemic forces constantly work to isolate and divide, creating similar pressures for Black communities, yet they still struggle to unite. While "going it alone" may work in some contexts, in hostile environments—both here and back home—it often leaves us vulnerable to forces that exploit our divisions.

While I admired Chris's independence, I wondered if not embracing collaboration meant missing out on something greater. In environments where unpredictability and hostility reign, working together isn't just about convenience—it's about survival. In both Africa and America, unity is the key to withstanding the challenges we face.

Theater Launched, Family Arrives, and a Break-In Shakes the Dream

With the theater project progressing, I needed to secure my house while managing construction. To address this, Chanda recommended her cousin for security. I built a small security post on the property and hired him to oversee the house, which let me focus entirely on the theater project.

I moved to an apartment across from the theater site to oversee the project firsthand. The first major task was constructing a tall perimeter wall to keep onlookers at bay and maintain privacy. Once the wall was complete, the ground was leveled. The real challenge arose with the appearance of venomous snakes on the site. To ensure the area's safety, I laid down plastic sheets and covered them with white gravel in hopes of deterring unwelcome wildlife.

As construction advanced, I built a small, compact home within the theater grounds to reduce living costs and remain on-site. The theater, envisioned as an open-air venue, was taking shape with a large white wall at the back to serve as a screen for the projector that would soon bring the project to life. A stage was built for multi-purpose events, enhancing the space's versatility. Progress was steady, but the town's atmosphere began to shift with the approaching presidential elections. Tension was rising, with an increasing sense of unease. Reports of political violence began to circulate, casting a shadow over the project and creating an unpredictable undercurrent that threatened momentum.

Amidst the mounting tension, my parents made their plans to visit me in Zambia, eager to check out my projects and experience my new life. I had been eagerly anticipating their arrival, but just as I was preparing for their visit, my house was broken into. The timing couldn't have been worse. After a quick investigation, suspicion fell on the recently dismissed workers, but what truly shook me was discovering that the security guard Chanda had recommended—her own cousin—was likely involved in the theft. It wasn't just the breach of trust that hit me; they had stolen valuables amounting to nearly $10,000, leaving me furious. The sheer loss, combined with the betrayal, felt like a punch to the gut, and the unsettling nature of it all weighed heavily on me, especially with my parents set to arrive. I knew I had to regain control of the situation before their arrival, but the sense of vulnerability lingered, making the stakes even higher.

Determined to ensure their safety and make their visit enjoyable, I decided to pause all further construction and booked them into the Radisson Blu, the top luxury hotel in Lusaka. The cost was high, but I wasn't willing to take any risks. I knew my parents had come to experience the best of Zambia, and I didn't want them exposed to the struggles and challenges I had been quietly dealing with—the scams, extortion, and the constant threat of something going wrong.

Their arrival was a moment of relief and excitement. They were enchanted with the Radisson Blu, especially their poolside room, and marveled at how affordable the luxury was compared to what they were used to. Yet, I remained vigilant, ever aware of the potential for scams and hidden dangers that they hadn't yet recognized. One day, I walked into their room to find about fifteen hotel staff members inside, supposedly helping with room service, but their attention on my parents' luggage made it clear they had other intentions. I swiftly ushered them out, though my parents believed they were just being helpful, lulled by the false smiles and gestures.

For our outings, I hired a trusted driver with police connections to ensure safe travels. On one trip, we were stopped and extorted by police officers, a common occurrence in Zambia. My parents were confused, still unfamiliar with the local dynamics. Despite these moments of tension, I focused on making their visit memorable.

The highlight was our safari at Chaminuka Park, which unfolded like a scene from a wildlife documentary. A heart-stopping moment came when a male lion pounced while we were taking photos, triggering a surreal chase involving cheetahs that had us quickly exiting the enclosure. Later, we traversed the savannah in a large truck, surrounded by zebras, wildebeests, and ostriches. My parents were especially delighted by a baby elephant and its mother, whom they got to pet and feed, making the experience even more magical.

Back at the hotel, we indulged in lavish dinners and meaningful conversations, but the constant presence of hotel staff became intrusive. Once they learned how much my parents had spent on their rooms, it seemed they were always lingering nearby, taking every chance to "help," which heightened my concern. To avoid this, I moved my parents to a beautiful condo in Ibex Hill, providing them with the privacy and comfort the hotel couldn't offer.

The shift to Ibex allowed us to finally relax, and during our stay, we stumbled upon Kingsland City, a billion-dollar project initiated by the Chinese to attract foreign investors. Kingsland City was a grand vision—a sprawling development that promised luxurious living for expatriates and wealthy locals. My parents were immediately drawn to the idea of owning a property in such a prime location, imagining a future there.

However, beneath the surface of this promising project, local African leaders and traditional villagers were quietly crafting a scheme. Under the guise of reclaiming "traditional land," they managed to halt the project entirely, asserting dubious land ownership claims. What had seemed like a golden investment opportunity quickly evaporated, leaving my parents disappointed by the hidden complexities of real estate in Africa. The abrupt end to Kingsland City served as a reminder of the challenges posed by local politics and the fragile nature of large-scale developments in the region.

A routine grocery shopping trip quickly turned uncomfortable as it felt like the entire store staff was watching our every move. This scrutiny made my parents uneasy, and it became clear that our full shopping cart was drawing more curiosity than we had anticipated. We decided that moving forward, we'd make smaller purchases to avoid standing out as much.

The constant requests for money outside the store further stressed my parents, giving them a firsthand look at the challenges I faced daily. Yet, these shared moments also brought us closer, strengthening our connection in this unfamiliar environment. As their visit came to an end after a month, I felt both proud and relieved. Despite the difficulties, I had managed to give them a real sense of my life in Zambia while keeping them safe and comfortable. Their departure was bittersweet, leaving me to reflect on how this visit had not only deepened our family bond but also reminded me of the resilience required to thrive in such a challenging place.

It was an unforgettable sight to see my parents and me together in the heart of the African savannah, feeding elephants—my mom's favorite animals. She had always dreamed of experiencing them up close, and my dad stood beside her, smiling and sharing in the joy of the moment. Watching them both revel in the experience, surrounded by these majestic creatures in their natural habitat, filled me with pride. It felt like we were sharing a moment that would last forever—one of those rare instances where a dream truly comes to life.

All Falls Down

With my parents safely back home, my full attention returned to the unresolved house break-in and the ongoing theater project. I rallied the construction crew, and work resumed with renewed vigor. To bolster security at my home, I reached out to Mwanza, hoping to rekindle our friendship. She and her sister agreed to stay at the house, providing much-needed vigilance and relief.

Meanwhile, the escalating unrest in South Africa, particularly in Johannesburg, worsened, prompting Prisca—my friend from Maboneng—to flee. Recognizing her potential and wanting to help, I offered her a position at the theater. Her hospitality experience, combined with her linguistic skills, added a vital layer of efficiency and local insight to our operations.

As the theater neared completion, I wanted to infuse the space with cultural vibrancy that reflected the community. I hired a mural painter to cover the walls with colorful depictions of African life, hoping the vibrant imagery would inspire creativity and a sense of belonging among the locals. However, just as I thought everything was on track, a significant problem arose.

The local electrical company demanded an exorbitant fee to connect power to the site—an amount so inflated that it felt like exploitation of my foreign status. Frustrated but undeterred, I opted for solar power. While functional, the solar system struggled under the demands of the projectors and kitchen appliances, leading to frequent interruptions that hindered my plans.

As I pressed on to complete the theater, my quest to identify the culprits behind the break-in intensified. The theft had cost me over $10,000 in valuables, and the emotional toll was weighing me down. When I approached the local police for assistance, they showed no interest. Frustrated, I pointed out that we were all Black, hoping to bridge the gap, but one officer coldly replied, "No, you're not one of us, you're a muzungu," refusing to help. Their blatant dismissal left me enraged.

Calling on my police contact from the safari, I managed to spur some action. Through his influence, we located the perpetrators hiding in the woods. However, despite catching them, the trial process was grueling and exposed the deep-rooted corruption within the judicial system. The prosecutor, initially cooperative after being bribed, began demanding more money. It felt as though justice itself was for sale, and with each passing day, my frustration grew.

The situation worsened when the family from whom I had purchased the land, along with the local village bushmen, began aggressively trying to reclaim it. Emboldened by the police's complacency, they launched a campaign to drive me out. The village chief even expressed his desire to take over my home and convert it into his palace. This was no idle threat; it was a coordinated effort to seize my property and assets under the guise of local entitlement.

I found myself in a battle for survival. Over $10 million worth of investments and resources were now at risk, and each day the stakes grew higher. What had started as a simple property purchase had turned into a fight for everything I had worked for. With every challenge and betrayal, my resolve hardened. I was determined not to lose it all. The lines between friend and foe had blurred, and every new face felt like a potential ally or a saboteur.

As tensions escalated to a boiling point, I realized this confrontation would either solidify my future in Zambia or bring everything crashing down. The battle wasn't just over land or property—it was about proving that I could stand my ground in a place where power and survival were constantly tested. The weight of it all pressed on me, but retreat wasn't an option. This was my moment to decide what legacy I would leave behind, and I was prepared to fight.

Greenwood Proposal

With the growing tensions surrounding me, I orchestrated a crucial meeting along Chailimbana Road, bringing together the wealthiest and most influential individuals in the region, including key members of the Soli Tribe. This gathering wasn't just about presenting a new business idea; it was an opportunity to solidify my foundation in Zambia by gaining the support of the region's top decision-makers and fostering solidarity with local leaders, hoping to ease some of the mounting pressure I had been facing.

My vision, inspired by the historic prosperity of Tulsa's Greenwood District—famously known as "Black Wall Street"—was bold and clear. I showcased videos of Greenwood's flourishing businesses before their tragic destruction, drawing parallels to what could be achieved in Chongwe. I emphasized how Black Americans in Greenwood had built a thriving community without relying on white society, and explained that Black Africans here had the same potential to replicate that success.

The plan centered on transforming the bustling stretch of Chailimbana Road into a vibrant commercial hub filled with shops, restaurants, and essential services that would revitalize the local economy. This would be a self-sustained, Black-led development capable of uplifting the entire community, breaking the cycle of dependence, and showcasing the true power of economic independence and collaboration.

I offered substantial financial backing, promising jobs, training, and a pathway to long-term growth. In my conversations with villagers outside the meeting, their desire for change was evident. They understood the potential this project held—new jobs, local businesses, and economic uplift that could dramatically alter the region's trajectory. For them, this wasn't just another business proposal; it was a chance to break the cycle of poverty and take control of their future.

However, inside the meeting with the wealthiest Africans in the region—the power players—there was an entirely different atmosphere. Despite the clear potential for significant economic growth, the leaders responded with an unexpected coldness. They showed no interest in creating a "Black Wall Street" or collaborating with the Black diaspora on such a project. Their rejection wasn't hesitant or cautious; it was firm and unequivocal. Even with the availability of open land along Chailimbana Road and the opportunity for transformative development, they dismissed the idea outright, indifferent to the benefits it could bring to their own community.

The leaders' indifference cast a chill over the room. Their refusal sharply contrasted with the enthusiasm I had seen from many of the villagers on the street, revealing a deep disconnect between the aspirations of the people and the closed-mindedness of their leaders.

This rejection was a heavy blow, not just to the project but to my broader efforts to establish something lasting in Zambia. I had hoped this meeting would be a pivotal moment, an opportunity to strengthen my foundation in the country with the support of its most influential figures. Instead, it became clear that the obstacles to progress were not just about resources but also about an unwillingness among the leaders to embrace change.

This experience dealt a significant blow to my ideal of Pan-Africanism, a vision I had long believed could unite Black people across the diaspora and the continent. Witnessing this ideal falter in real time, I was confronted by the indifference of leaders who had the power to help but chose not to. It forced me to question whether Pan-Africanism could truly thrive when those in power were unwilling to act in the best interest of their own people and showed little interest in Black unity.

Their decision reflected a deeper issue. Despite the clear benefits the project could bring, the leaders prioritized their own status over fostering progress for the broader community. This wasn't just a simple refusal; it was a rejection of solidarity, revealing a gap between the hopes of the people and the self-preservation of those in power.

This moment forced me to confront a tough reality: even the best-laid plans can be derailed by those unwilling to embrace change. It wasn't merely about the practical hurdles of building something in Africa; it was about the deeply rooted attitudes that obstruct real progress.

Though disheartening, this setback only strengthened my resolve. The refusal to support a transformative project for their own people was a hard pill to swallow, but it reminded me that change is never easy, and the road ahead would be long. No matter how difficult, I was more determined than ever to keep pushing for local empowerment and progress, even if I had to fight for every inch of it.

Shockwaves Throughout The Community

Malola, the small village in the Chongwe district where my main home was located, was becoming ground zero for a storm of conflicts that would soon escalate into what came to be known as the Malola Wars. My properties, once a beacon of hope and promise, were now under constant threat. The looming danger was undeniable, forcing me to take extreme security measures just to protect myself and what I had built. The air in Malola grew heavier with each passing day, as violence slowly gripped the region, and whispers of conflict turned into deafening cries for survival.

At the same time, the broader Black expatriate community across Africa was rocked by a series of brutal, targeted attacks. It became clear that being a foreigner—particularly a Black American or Black British expatriate—had become increasingly perilous. News of violent assaults targeting women spread quickly. Numerous Black American and Black British women were among those killed, their deaths a cruel reminder of how vulnerable expatriates had become. These attacks sent a ripple of fear through our community, forcing everyone to heighten their vigilance.

Africa, once seen as a sanctuary, was beginning to reveal a darker, more dangerous side. The dream of a welcoming ancestral home was giving way to a harsh reality, one filled with violence and uncertainty. For many of us, the idea of Africa as a safe refuge was being replaced by a landscape fraught with peril and distrust. The events unfolding in Malola were a stark testament to this shift, marking a period defined by resilience and the constant need for survival.

In Gambia alone, six Black women expats were brutally murdered, sparking fear and outrage throughout the diaspora community. The violence didn't stop there. The Gambian Minister of Land issued a directive urging citizens not to sell land to Black Americans, Black British, or Black Caribbeans, labeling them as "land grabbers." Meanwhile, Arab, white, and Asian investors faced no such restrictions. This blatant discrimination shook the expatriate community, fueling anger and a deep sense of betrayal.

The violence wasn't confined to Gambia. In Ghana, an elderly Black woman and her daughter were butchered after winning a land dispute, in an incident eerily similar to my own struggles in Zambia. In Tanzania, a Black woman was dragged behind a car during a robbery, her skin scraped to the bone.

Single Black women in Africa were especially vulnerable, lacking the protective structures they might have relied on in America or Europe. Black men weren't spared either, often falling victim to poisoning or violent attacks. My friend, doing business in Nigeria, faced this harsh reality firsthand when he was attacked by a mob after refusing to pay extortion. He barely escaped with his life, running over several attackers as he fled in his car.

These chilling incidents fundamentally altered the way many Black Americans perceived Africa. The sense of connection to the continent was still strong, but it was tempered by the realization that it came with its own dangers. The rising hostility towards Black expatriates was undeniable.
It was becoming clear that Africa was no longer the safe haven many of us had envisioned.

This wave of violence wasn't just isolated to a few countries—it reflected a larger shift in the relationship between the African diaspora and the continent itself. For me, these events revealed deeper, more unsettling truths about Africa's fragile balance between hospitality and hostility. The same nations that called for the Black diaspora to return home seemed, in many cases, unprepared to welcome us safely. It wasn't just a betrayal by individual actors; it hinted at something much more insidious, with whispers of white supremacy subtly influencing these violent actions.

The promises of Africa as a sanctuary had given way to a harsher reality, and for many, the idea of "homecoming" had become a dangerous gamble—death waiting for some upon arrival. It felt like the ground was shifting beneath our feet, as if the continent was being pulled in different directions, both welcoming and rejecting us at the same time.

In hindsight, these events became a reckoning, forcing me to reevaluate my role and expectations in Africa. The battles I would soon face in Malola were no longer just personal struggles—they were a microcosm of a much larger conflict between Black expatriates and the challenges of truly finding belonging on the continent. What happened next in Malola would not only test my resolve but fundamentally reshape how I saw Africa, and how it saw me.

With my resources and connections, I organized a meeting with the wealthiest Africans in the area and showed them videos of the Greenwood District in the 1920–50s. My intention was not only to demonstrate my solidarity with the people and ease growing tensions but to inspire the recreation of such a thriving community. However, I was appalled by their lack of interest. Despite living in a land that was entirely theirs, free from the direct threat of white supremacy, they showed no solidarity in recreating a Black Wall Street in Africa. It was disheartening to see that the vision of building something powerful for future generations didn't resonate with them, despite the immense potential they held in their hands.

Malola Wars

Amid rising tensions with local law enforcement and regional chiefs, my once-promising venture in Zambia had quickly devolved into a fight for survival. The stakes were far higher than I'd ever imagined, and walking away from my investments wasn't an option. The only path forward was to take drastic action. I made a choice I never thought I'd have to—I armed myself. I purchased a rifle from a Middle Eastern dealer, an act that felt crucial for securing my safety as the situation escalated. The deal opened my eyes to the deep-rooted corruption in the region, especially when a neighboring chief exploited a loophole, trading hunting rights for guns despite the ban on firearm sales during the election period. It was a reminder of how easily those in power could twist the rules in their favor.

But the rifle alone wasn't enough. In a daring move, I turned to Chinese merchants to buy explosives, knowing it would take more than just firearms to defend what I had built. The transaction was risky, but it felt like the only way to truly fortify my position. Each step I took brought me closer to the inevitable confrontation that seemed to be looming on the horizon.

The tension thickened by the day, and it finally snapped one late afternoon when my phone rang. Mwanza's panicked voice cut through the static: "They're setting fire to the property!" she screamed, chaos crackling in the background.

Chris and I jumped into action, racing back to the house as fast as the car would allow. But nothing could have prepared us for the horror that awaited us.

Flames devoured the walls, thick smoke choked the air, and the once-solid perimeter fence lay in smoldering ruins. The security post was obliterated, and the crops—my pride and hard work—lay in ruins, charred beyond recognition. My water tank, once a vital resource, had melted into a grotesque heap of twisted metal. Even parts of the house had succumbed to the inferno, the fire greedily consuming what was left of my sanctuary.

This wasn't just vandalism; it was an assault. The intensity of the attack felt eerily familiar, like the racial violence of the Klan against my ancestors, now playing out on African soil—against me. Mwanza, trapped inside the house, had barely escaped the flames. When I went to the local headman for help, his laughter echoed in my ears, confirming what I had already suspected—he was involved. His nonchalant attitude revealed the depth of the betrayal.

Chris and I knew we couldn't rely on anyone but ourselves. He moved into the house, and together we fortified our position. To strengthen our defenses, we bought two dogs: a purebred German Shepherd and a Boerboel mix, both renowned for their skill in bush environments. Their presence added a layer of security, knowing they'd be invaluable in detecting any threats lurking nearby.

In gratitude for their loyalty and service, I helped Mwanza and her sister start a business in town, especially after Mwanza's near-death experience during the fire. It was the least I could do to repay them for their bravery.

Our daily lives soon morphed into a survival routine. Sniper training and combat drills became our new normal as we prepared for the next attack. The enemy was always out there, waiting. One day, while scouting the land through the rifle scope, we spotted a man crawling through the woods, spying on us. The moment we confronted him, he bolted, but the message was clear: we were being hunted.

The nights were tense, the darkness amplifying our sense of vulnerability. Intruders took advantage of the cover, their presence betrayed only by the faint rustling of leaves. I had no choice but to throw explosives in their direction—a drastic but necessary move to scatter them and protect what was ours. The threat was constant, and it was clear we were being relentlessly targeted.

By day, the menace didn't fade. Villagers would slowly pass by the house, their eyes full of malice. They pretended not to look, but their glances lingered just long enough to send a clear message. Sometimes, we'd find spitting cobras deliberately placed near the property—a silent yet deadly warning. The hostility surrounded us, no matter the hour.

As the situation worsened and villagers began encroaching on Chris's land, it became evident that our decision to build separately—dividing our resources—was creating unexpected challenges. The physical distance between us made it harder to respond quickly when issues arose, leaving both properties more vulnerable. To address the immediate risks, Chris constructed a high wall around his land, but it was clear that this was only a temporary fix to a larger issue. In an environment as unpredictable as this, working apart left us exposed.

The danger didn't only come from the villagers. The police checkpoint near Chris's home had transformed into an extortion racket, far worse than anything I'd ever experienced in Zambia. Their harassment was relentless, with bribes demanded at every turn. This financial drain compounded the strain we were already under, making survival feel like a battle on all fronts.

Through it all, the lesson was clear: we needed to work together more closely to survive. Building separately had left gaps in our security, exposing us to both external threats and internal pressures. In this unpredictable environment, unity wasn't just an ideal—it was essential. I realized why the Chinese and other communities maintained close ties, standing side by side. It wasn't merely a matter of convenience; their collective strength forged a robust defense, a vital element that we had sacrificed by choosing to go our separate ways.

157

Our daily existence became warlike. Trust was reserved for those within our tight circle, and isolation was a necessity. Tension escalated when Chris was poisoned—an attack that nearly took his life. From that moment on, we prepared every meal ourselves, refusing to rely on anyone else. Poisoning had become a real threat, and the stakes had never been higher.

With each passing day, the headman's role in the escalating conflict became increasingly clear. He was orchestrating the attacks, rallying the villagers to target us. What had started as a land dispute had transformed into a fight for survival. Each day tested our endurance as we fought to maintain our right to live securely in this hostile environment. The stakes were no longer merely about property; they were about life and death. What had once been a business investment now felt like a war, forcing us to confront the brutal reality of our situation.

The realization hit hard: in a place like this, independence wasn't enough. Survival demanded unity, constant vigilance, and the willingness to trust those closest to us. We had been operating as individuals, but now it was clear that only collective strength could see us through this relentless struggle.

Everything I had worked for was now up in flames, and my friend Mwanza had barely escaped with her life. My exotic crops, which had taken a considerable time to cultivate, were being destroyed alongside my entire water system. An unimaginable amount of wealth was being reduced to ash before my eyes. Anger surged through me, as fierce and consuming as the flames themselves. This wasn't just a loss—it was a declaration of war, and someone was going to pay.

The African bushmen, the dwellers of the outskirts, had evolved into the deadliest of foes. Armed with an unmatched mastery of the land and the art of poison, they became the backbone of the Headman's army, their cunning treachery a constant threat. Their ingenuity in warfare was terrifying; they even unleashed poisonous snakes as silent weapons of death. They watched my home day and night, hidden deep within the bushes, their eyes cold and calculating, always waiting for the perfect moment to strike. Their relentless and unpredictable nature left me with only one option: to stay vigilant, knowing that every second could mean the difference between life and death.

Our two dogs, Abashai—the German Shepherd—and Hannibal—the Boerboel—were more than just protection; they were essential to our survival. Trained by Chris, they could detect poisoned food left by bushmen, a tactic used to eliminate guard dogs before striking. We had heard of a Black woman in Ghana who lost her dogs to this same method before being killed herself. Hannibal and Abashai weren't merely barking at shadows—they sensed danger before it even reached us, alerting us to intruders hiding in the thick bush. In a place where trust was a rare commodity, those two dogs were the only ones, aside from Chris, I could truly count on. In Africa, it wasn't just about loyalty—it was about staying alive.

Village Eyes

During this volatile period, I took decisive action to fortify my defenses by creating a covert group called "Village Eyes." This network was made up of locals who had grown weary of the corruption and hardship that shaped their lives. They had long suffered under a broken system and were ready to fight back. Their anger was undeniable, and their willingness to stand with me came from a shared desire for change. They didn't just see my struggle—they lived it. This was the same battle they had fought for years, against the very forces that had repeatedly failed them.

Each member was chosen carefully, knowing that their deep distrust of the authorities made them invaluable in this volatile environment. Their insider knowledge was crucial, keeping me informed of escalating tensions within the village and the government's underhanded tactics. It wasn't long before word spread that the government planned to target foreign-owned businesses through sabotage and extortion, starting with Rwandan and Congolese entrepreneurs.

A troubling pattern emerged—African expatriates were being singled out, while white- and Asian-owned businesses remained untouched. The message was clear: it was only a matter of time before they came for me. Sensing the growing danger, I made a calculated decision to transfer all my assets into Prisca's name, leveraging her Zambian identity to shield them from government interference.

Alongside securing my assets, I reached out to trusted friends in Lusaka, investing in their ventures to expand my protective circle. By building a stronger network around me, I didn't just fortify my own defenses—I created a community that would stand with me when the time came.

The streets were no longer safe, and I became more cautious, confining myself within the fortified walls of my estate while my network kept watch. Yet, even with these precautions, the violation of my home gnawed at me. It wasn't just the financial blow—over $105,000 worth of property destroyed in the fire—or the loss of the agricultural systems I had built. This was personal. My sanctuary had been breached, and the security I had worked so hard to create was shattered. The anger simmered, and the need for retribution became a necessity.

The losses weren't just about money or possessions; they represented an attack on everything I was trying to build. This wasn't just a random strike—it was an assault on my vision, and I knew I couldn't let it go unanswered. From that moment, every move became calculated, precise. It wasn't just about survival anymore—it was about making sure those responsible would pay. I wasn't going to be defeated, and anyone who dared to challenge me would face the consequences.

Kill The Headman

Amid the escalating land disputes, I found myself locked in a relentless battle at the village court, squaring off against the headman's delegates. Each confrontation felt like a high-stakes chess match, and every legal victory only intensified the animosity from local leadership. To protect myself during these tense moments, I was never alone, always bringing a group of close allies to reinforce my presence. While the court rulings secured my rights on paper, they deepened the hostility on the ground. The headman and his inner circle retaliated subtly, their influence looming over the daily operations of my newly completed movie theater. With the building still plagued by electricity issues, the challenges kept mounting.

It became clear that playing by the rules of the court wasn't enough. The headman and his allies wielded a different kind of power—one rooted in tradition and beyond the reach of legal victories. If I didn't act decisively, my vision for a thriving business and a stable life in Zambia could be crushed before it even began. I knew I had to cut the problem off at its source.

I traveled to Lusaka, seeking advice from my trusted police contact. This time, I wasn't looking for bureaucratic solutions—I needed a force that operated outside the law, a team capable of precision. My contact arranged a secretive meeting with C5, a special unit known for its ruthless efficiency—the Zambian equivalent of a SWAT team. Under the cover of night, we met at a secluded location, far from prying eyes.

The plan was clear but dangerous: I offered 12,000 Kwacha for a covert strike on the headman and his closest allies. This wasn't just a scare tactic; it was about eliminating the source of the problem. The headman's influence had poisoned everything I'd worked to build, and the only way forward was to remove him entirely. We crafted a meticulous, tightly held plan—no leaks, no errors. The stakes were too high, and caution had gotten us nowhere.

As the day of the operation approached, tension thickened, but I pressed forward with unwavering focus. There was no turning back now. Whatever the outcome, I was prepared to face it head-on, knowing the cost of doing nothing was far greater than the risk we were about to take. It was time to eliminate the headman.

I waited in position, tense but resolute, knowing the moment for action had come. The plan had been meticulously crafted, every detail accounted for. The risks were enormous, but after all I had lost, I no longer cared. I was ready, fully prepared for whatever lay ahead, regardless of the consequences. The night was thick with anticipation as I waited for the others to arrive, my mind sharp, my resolve unshaken.

Then, just as the mission was set to unfold, word came that C5 had pulled out, citing "unforeseen complications." The excuse left me seething. All the tension, all the preparation—it suddenly felt like it had been for nothing.

Chris, ever the pragmatist, saw this as a sign—a warning that the path we were on was too dangerous. His words didn't shake me. I had come too far, and the weight of the money I'd lost was heavier than any potential fallout. The risks seemed meaningless compared to everything I had sacrificed.

But with C5 out, there was no way to move forward. Reluctantly, I agreed to halt the operation, though the anger still simmered beneath the surface. I knew I needed time to rethink my strategy.

The fury still simmered beneath the surface, and I wasn't ready to let go. Since I couldn't reach the people I truly wanted, my attention shifted to their children, who often wandered near my land, unattended. With the Chongwe River nearby, I knew just the place where they could vanish without a trace.

But even as the anger boiled inside me, I pulled back, realizing I needed to regroup and rethink my strategy. The operation was on hold, but the fight was far from over. The battle had merely been postponed, and I would be ready to strike when the time was right.

Feeling the pressure mounting, I decided to take a brief break in Lusaka. I left the theater in Prisca's capable hands, while she fine-tuned the menu, and checked into a quiet hotel to clear my head. This short retreat gave me a much-needed moment of calm amidst the chaos, allowing me to step back from the whirlwind of conflicts and decisions. It reminded me how crucial it was to carefully navigate the treacherous landscape of local politics and power dynamics. This wasn't just a break; it was a vital opportunity to reassess my strategy as I prepared for my next moves in the complex game of influence and control in Zambia.

During this harrowing period, I found myself locked in a battle with Headman Kapini, a man who wielded his power with chilling ruthlessness. As village headman, his duty was to lead, but instead, he declared war on me. He coveted my house, seeing it as the perfect palace for his ambitions. Using his authority to extort and intimidate, Kapini made my life unbearable, pushing me to the edge, determined to force me out of my own home. But as his aggressions grew, so did my resolve. I could no longer just defend—I had to act. It was time to confront him head-on and put an end to his tyranny once and for all.

The Village Eyes became my lifeline. I couldn't be everywhere at once, and the language barrier was a constant hurdle. But this organization was my link to survival, blending into the shadows alongside the police and bushmen who stalked the outskirts. Every move they made kept me two steps ahead of danger. This wasn't just vigilance—it was war. The threat loomed constantly, but one thing was clear: even in the darkest, most desperate moments, there were allies I could count on. Their silent work in the shadows wasn't just keeping me informed—it was keeping me alive.

Furious over losses exceeding $100,000, I was consumed by a thirst for revenge. My anger drove me to reconnect with my police contact, who introduced me to Zambia's infamous C5 unit. Together, we devised a clandestine plan to strike back and cut the head off the snake. This wasn't a small operation—it had the potential to escalate into an international incident, even drawing the attention of the U.S. Embassy. But at that moment, I didn't care. There was no way I was going to let someone burn my property to the ground without facing consequences. This was personal, and I was ready for war.

A Devastating Phone Call

Lusaka's upscale neighborhoods offered me a brief, welcome escape from the storm brewing in my life. I indulged in simple pleasures—fine dining, a few drinks—savoring rare moments of peace. One evening, after spending time with a charming student from the University of Zambia, a fierce rainstorm swept through. The rhythmic pounding of rain against the windows mirrored the turmoil I carried inside. But little did I know, that storm would pale in comparison to the one about to strike my heart.

Everything changed with a single phone call that night. My parents' trembling voices delivered news I wasn't prepared for—my mother was gravely ill, with only weeks left to live. The doctor's words landed like a blow: "If you want to see her again, you need to come now." The weight of those words sank deep, but there was no decision to make. I had to be by her side.

Yet, the timing couldn't have been worse. I was in the final stages of overseeing a million-dollar project in Zambia, with millions in assets tied up. I knew I couldn't leave the properties unattended, not with everything hanging in the balance. My heart was with my mother, but the stakes here were enormous. It felt like everything I had built, everything I had fought so hard for, was unraveling at once. My mind spun, torn between the urgency of family and the looming responsibilities on the ground. It was a collision of two worlds—personal and professional—leaving me to grapple with an impossible choice.

For two agonizing days, I struggled with the decision. Every part of me was torn between the life I had built in Africa and the life I had left behind. I walked the streets of Lusaka and Chongwe, searching for clarity, but instead, something inside me broke. The idealism of Pan-Africanism that had once driven me was crumbling before my eyes. Africa no longer appeared as a place of shared Black identity or solidarity. Instead, I saw corruption, chaos, and a people who cared nothing for the unity I had imagined.

Where I had once looked for brotherhood, I found only betrayal. The people I had hoped would stand with me had shown only greed and deception. They weren't my allies—they were my enemies. The dream of unity I had clung to now felt like a cruel joke, and bitterness surged within me like a fire I couldn't extinguish.

As I walked through streets filled with people lost in their own struggle, resigned to a life of stagnation, the contrast between what I had hoped for and the harsh reality that surrounded me hit harder than I could bear. Pan-Africanism wasn't just an empty dream—it was a lie I had carried for too long. And it took the news of my mother's impending death to finally tear it away.

With every step, the realization sank deeper: I wasn't one of them. I wasn't African—I was a Black American, and the gulf between us was too wide to cross. My pride, once rooted in the belief in unity, now twisted into anger, slicing through the illusions I had dragged across continents. My place wasn't here, in this land of false brotherhood. My place was with my family, with my mother.

The raw truth hit hard, shattering any remaining hope I had held. The dream was dead, and the only thing left was my need to go home.

With a heavy heart, I made the difficult decision to leave Zambia behind. I reached out to an African woman leader I trusted—someone who, while not fully aligned with my vision, understood the weight of being Black in a global context. I sold her the theater and several other properties. The process was rushed and painful, but I had no choice. My mother's health was rapidly declining, and I knew I had to be with her before it was too late.

The community that had depended on the jobs and opportunities I created was left in disarray. Over 300 workers, both direct and contracted, suddenly found themselves facing an uncertain future. The corruption I had battled for so long had finally forced my hand. Staying any longer would pull me deeper into a fight I could no longer afford to wage. My mind was focused on one thing—getting home to my family.

In those final days, I grappled with the weight of my decision. I said my goodbyes, starting with Prisca, offering her a generous sum for her loyalty and support. Each farewell wasn't just a parting of ways—it was a severing of the dream I had once poured so much into. As I packed my belongings and arranged my flight back to the U.S., the reality of leaving Zambia sank in. I knew my sudden departure would leave a void in the lives of those who had worked alongside me, and the weight of that realization was heavy. But I couldn't stay—I had to be with my mother in her final days.

What struck me most was the faces of my employees, the ones I had hoped to uplift. In the end, the same leaders who sought to drive me out only succeeded in harming their own people. That bitter truth lingered as I prepared to leave, knowing they would have to navigate a system designed to fail them.

Even though I trusted the woman who bought the theater to carry on my vision, that trust was quickly broken. She wasted no time painting over the murals symbolizing African pride and history, covering them with plain white paint. The villagers, many of whom had helped create the artwork and felt deeply connected to it, were stunned. What had been a vibrant celebration of Black identity was erased, leaving only blank, soulless walls where culture once thrived.

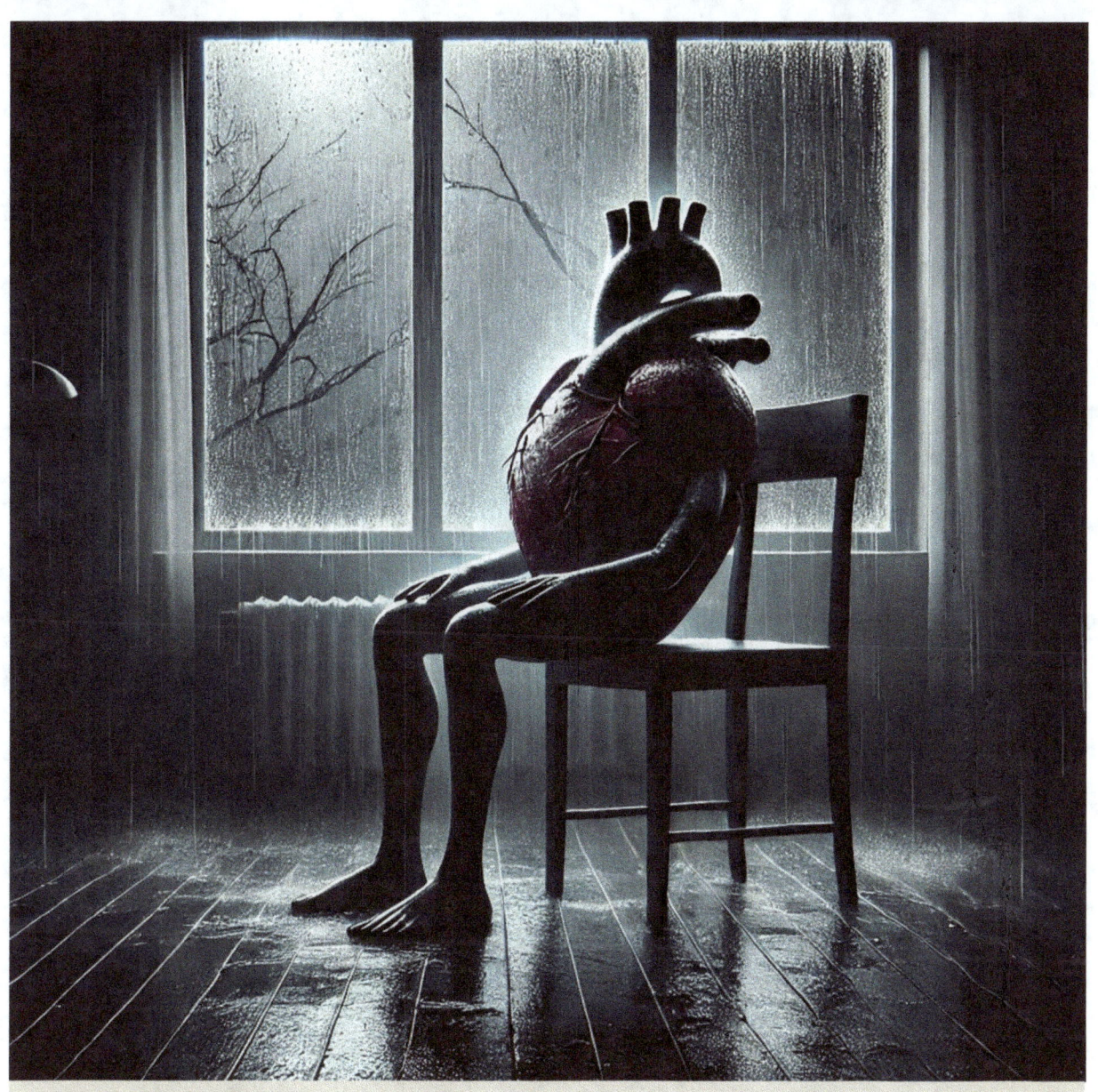

After the devastating phone call, my body was lifeless on the bed, but my heart—ripped out—sat by the window, watching the treacherous storm unfold. The loneliness, the cold wind cutting through me, felt unbearable. Hearing devastation was one thing, but being 10,000 miles away, wondering if I'd ever see my mother again—that was a torment worse than hell itself. Every gust of wind seemed to carry my despair, pulling me deeper into the abyss of uncertainty. There was no escape from the storm inside or out.

As I walked through the town, taking in the faces of those around me, disgust churned deep within me. The illusion of Pan-African unity had shattered completely, leaving me to see Africa for what it truly was—backward, divided, and utterly hopeless. There was no black solidarity here, only betrayal and backstabbing. The decision was clear now, almost too easy; I had to get out of this place. This was no motherland; it was, in fact, motherless. My mother—my true connection—was back home, on my own land. It was time to leave. Immediately. There was nothing left for me here.

The True Adversaries

With Chris still in Zambia, he took charge of selling my remaining properties—an invaluable help, as managing this from America would have been impossible. It was a somber farewell, knowing I was leaving him to navigate the treacherous terrain of Africa alone. Still, he assured me he could handle what remained of my legacy there.

Packed and ready, I headed to the airport for my flight home via Dubai. Then came the final blow: despite having all the necessary documents, the airport staff detained me, confiscated my passport, and demanded $1,000 if I wanted to leave the country. Desperation clawed at me as I tried to explain—my mother was dying—but their cold, dismissive response hit me like a slap. "We don't care," they said, their indifference chilling me to the core. That moment, more than anything before, was the final straw. It shattered any lingering illusions I had about this place—a land I had once viewed as a sanctuary.

Trapped and helpless, I watched as time slipped away, and I missed my flight. I contacted Chris and Prisca, who rushed to gather the ransom for my release. Ten agonizing hours dragged by as I sat there, powerless. A Chinese man sat beside me, caught in the same extortion scheme. The officials mockingly called him "China man," and as I watched their cruelty unfold, I couldn't help but think—I couldn't wait until the Chinese recolonized the Africans. These people had no respect for their own land, no vision for its potential. They were squandering everything and didn't deserve it.

After what felt like an eternity, Chris and Prisca arrived with the money. Still, the airport staff hesitated to return my passport, pushing my patience to its absolute limit. Only when I threatened to involve the U.S. embassy did they finally back down. I snatched my passport, booked another flight—this time to South Africa—and made it out, eventually transferring smoothly through Doha and heading home.

As I boarded that final flight, the bitter irony of my journey hit me. I had left America to escape racial tensions, only to find myself ensnared in a far more insidious form of racism in an all-Black nation. This ordeal didn't just signify the collapse of my African dream; it shattered my previous understanding of where the true threats to my freedom and dignity could lie.

No Hugs For Homecoming

Now back in America, I arrived just in time to be with my mom during her final days. For those precious weeks before she passed, I was by her side. I was there for her last breath, cherishing every moment we had together. It was a bittersweet gift—one that reminded me I had made the right choice in putting family over business. Yet, as much as those moments gave me solace, returning home also plunged me into a downward spiral of stress. I found escape in heavy drinking, numbing myself through frequent blackouts in public spaces, trying to silence the storm inside me.

One chaotic night at a local bar, my emotions boiled over. I overheard a Ghanaian woman, gushing about her country, praising it like it was the greatest place on earth. The memories of my time in Africa—the betrayal, the anger—surged up, and before I knew it, I shot back, "You mean that shit hole of a country?" The words came out with venom, sparking a heated argument. The room shifted. A heated argument erupted, and to my disbelief, even local Black Americans— most of whom had never even set foot in Africa—sided with her. As they pushed me out, the rage surged inside me, burning hotter with each step. It hit me hard—no matter where I went, I didn't truly belong.

That incident deepened my depression, fueling a profound sense of displacement. Meanwhile, Chris had managed to finalize the sale and distribution of our remaining properties in Zambia, ensuring that we honored those who had truly stood by us. As a gesture of gratitude, we gifted the remaining unsold properties to the African allies who had offered unwavering support during our hardest times. Not long after, Chris too left Africa, officially closing the chapter on our shared dreams. The sense of finality was overwhelming, as the vision we once had for a lasting legacy in Africa faded into distant memories.

Back home, I spent my days drinking and wandering aimlessly, reflecting on how a once hopeful dream had turned into a nightmare. Yet, I had accomplished what I set out to do—discover if Black Americans could truly thrive in Africa, and the answer to that question lies within these pages. There were good times, but the bad far outweighed them—something most visitors wouldn't fully grasp, but I had lived it for four long years. I returned stronger, with a deeper understanding of my lineage—the strongest in the world, Black American lineage. I no longer saw myself as a representative of Africa, and the first step in moving on was letting go, discarding all my African artifacts. It was time to leave the past behind and start anew.

Lessons Learned / Best African Country

The most important lesson for any Black American traveling to —or especially moving to—Africa is this: never arrive thinking you're one of them. You are American, and their culture isn't yours. These are not your people, and they are certainly not your brothers and sisters. If you go there believing you're "returning home," trying to connect in a desperate attempt for belonging, they will see it—and they will exploit it. Black Americans are not Africans, and knowing this is your strongest shield against the countless schemes waiting for you in the motherless land.

Don't be misled by your brief visit; the smiles and friendly gestures you encountered were only surface-level. A week simply isn't enough time to uncover what truly lies beneath. The real intentions start to emerge only after the initial warmth fades—once you've stayed long enough for the masks to fall.

For Black American women, you're even more of a target because you don't have the same protection you do in the States. Back home, Black women can carry themselves however they choose, but outside the U.S., that freedom isn't tolerated. In certain places, an attitude that might be brushed off in America can get you jailed or even beaten. I've personally seen Black American women locked up for their attitude, so keep that in mind. And more importantly, don't fall for love schemes. Many Africans specialize in deceit and manipulation, and they can easily entice a woman into believing she's found love. If they can make millions of dollars running these scams online, imagine how much easier it is to do it in person. Stay sharp, and don't let yourself get played.

For those daring enough to do business in Africa, especially if you plan to stay for a while, it's crucial to stick to the city, where most resources are concentrated. The cities may be poorly managed and chaotic, but venturing into the villages presents a subtle yet significant danger that many underestimate. If you're on your own, align yourself with Africans who reject corrupt governments and genuinely believe in Black unity. These individuals are rare, but they stand out—it won't be hard to identify them in a population that tends to follow predictable patterns.

When investing in local businesses, focus on small stakes and joint ventures only. Avoid pouring all your energy into running a business alone in Africa. By owning just 10% of a venture, you limit your exposure to a fraction of the potential issues—legal fees, corrupt schemes, and most critically, the risk of nationalization.

The biggest threat for a Black American doing business in Africa is the possibility of the government nationalizing your assets, leaving you with nothing. Always remember, you're not African, and they know it. You'll be treated differently, with less regard for your rights than white or Asian business owners. Don't be discouraged by how easily these groups seem to progress—they benefit from privileges and protections that won't be extended to you. Understand the environment, play it smart, but always keep in mind the unique challenges you'll face.

Focus your efforts near the upscale malls and universities—these areas attract the most progressive, modern-minded Africans. When pitching your ideas, expect quick enthusiasm; they're hungry for change and seize opportunities much faster than you might expect in the U.S. While this eagerness can be a good sign, don't rush. Take your time to vet potential partners thoroughly to avoid future pitfalls.

Black American and Black European women should avoid traveling to villages alone, especially when dealing with land disputes or other sensitive matters. Sadly, there have been too many cases of Black women being murdered while fighting for land in Africa. This is not a place where you can navigate such challenges solo. In environments like this, where the risks are high and the dynamics often treacherous, it is essential to have a trusted male companion for protection and support when venturing into villages or rural areas.

The name of the game for many Africans is to watch you pour your resources into building your home or business, cultivating the land, while they circle like vultures, waiting for you to finish so they can take it. They'll pull every scheme in the book—most often claiming the land was theirs all along and they didn't know who sold it to you. And this only happens after all the hard work is done. The word for the day in Africa is "pleonexia"—the insatiable desire to possess what others have. Don't fall for the sad stories Africans will throw at you either. They'll stoop to low tactics, often claiming they need money for funerals or, more commonly, for medicine, all designed to make you feel sorry for them—but don't fall for it.

If you're doing business with other Black Americans, make sure your team is united. Individualistic mindsets won't work in Africa— you need a solid team. The biggest challenge with Black Americans in business is their tendency to want to do things alone. Many would rather struggle independently than push forward together. Make sure everyone is on the same page and committed to a collective effort.

Living arrangements are key. Everyone should live in the same compound or no more than literally 1 minute apart for safety reasons. If the Chinese can do it and succeed, so can Black Americans. Stay in the city where the resources are, and if you need to venture into the villages or the bush, keep your time there brief.
Success in Africa requires strategy, unity, and careful planning

—this isn't the place for lone wolves.

When it comes to the best country in Africa for a Black American or diaspora to live, travel, or do business, South Africa stands out as the most optimal choice. While the entire continent offers unique experiences, South Africa provides a combination of factors that make it more comfortable and accessible for those coming from Western countries.

A key reason is South Africa's deep understanding of racism, shaped by its history with apartheid and extreme economic disparities between Black and white South Africans. Black South Africans often relate to the experiences of Black Americans and are more likely to sympathize with them in racial matters. On contrary, other African nations, ironically, may side with white people on issues of race, making South Africa a more welcoming environment for Black expatriates.

South Africa's infrastructure also sets it apart. With modern cities, paved roads, and reliable services, it offers a level of development that mirrors what Black Americans and Black Europeans are used to. This infrastructure—along with familiar business systems like stock markets, fixed prices, and installment plans—makes settling in and doing business far easier compared to countries with less developed systems. Even though white Afrikaaners still dominate commerce, their presence ensures that the business environment feels familiar and structured, easing the transition for Black expatriates.

That said, South Africa isn't without its problems. Crime rates in certain areas, especially in major cities, can be extremely high and serve as a major deterrent. In places like Zambia, Ghana, or Botswana while the infrastructure might be lacking, day-to-day life can feel much safer than even the safest neighborhoods in the U.S. The danger in those countries isn't necessarily in walking around or going about your daily life—it's when you start doing business that real risks emerge. In conclusion, while no African country is without challenges, South Africa offers the most familiar, economically viable, and supportive environment for Black Americans and Black Europeans, balancing African culture with Western expectations and providing unique safety, opportunity, and understanding.

Ultimately, Black Americans owe Africans nothing. For centuries, we've been the only Black group on the planet consistently fighting for Blackness on a global scale, yet we've received little to no respect from the broader diaspora. We fought to liberate Ethiopia preventing Africa from being completely colonized, helped build Africa's first airlines, stood on the front lines against apartheid, and even paved the way for Africans to come to the United States. Black Americans have done more than enough to keep Pan-Africanism alive. And in return, we've been met with nothing but resentment.

From my own journey in Africa and the experiences of countless other Black Americans, it's become glaringly clear: Pan-Africanism is a one-sided deal—one that Africans and Caribbeans themselves have abandoned. The idea that we share a united struggle, a common purpose, is a fantasy we've been fed for far too long. The truth is, Africans see us as outsiders, and our efforts to connect and build bridges have been met with indifference or even contempt.

I've never felt more powerful than I do now, after fully embracing my Black American identity and accepting that Pan-Africanism, in its idealized form, is a myth. It's a disease that has plagued Black Americans, making us believe we need to fight for people who don't like us. We are stronger fighting for our rights at home, where the real battle is, instead of trying to save people who don't care to return the favor. It's time for Black Americans to cure themselves of this delusion. Stick with the devil you know—because the one you don't is already sharpening their knife behind your back.

Pan Africanism Is Dead......

Lioness Force Field

What ultimately kept me alive during my time in Zambia wasn't brute strength or careful planning—it was a deep understanding of human nature, drawn from both observation and instinct. Over time, it became clear that the greatest danger wasn't the environment or wildlife, but the men I had once trusted. The more successful I became, the more I felt the weight of their jealousy and resentment. There's something inherent in men that drives them to compete, to feel threatened by another man's success. It was an unfortunate reality I couldn't afford to ignore, so I made a pivotal decision: I surrounded myself with women, empowering them in business and even entrusting them with my security.

What I discovered was striking. Unlike men, women didn't respond to my achievements with envy or a desire to undermine me. They embraced the success, working alongside me rather than against me. This mirrored a dynamic I had observed in the African wild. A male lion's strength isn't in his solitary power but in the lionesses who surround him. They are the hunters, the nurturers, and the protectors of the pride, while the male takes care of the larger tasks, such as defending the territory. They are disciplined, loyal, and efficient, allowing him to thrive. This became the model I needed to follow.

The women around me became my protectors, my allies, and my partners. They managed the land, crafted medicines, negotiated deals, and kept a watchful eye on local threats, while I funded and managed the entire operation. Their loyalty became my most valuable resource, ensuring my safety and success in ways the men never could. They handled everything with a focus and dedication that allowed me to thrive in an otherwise hostile environment.

This shift wasn't just a survival tactic—it became a blueprint for navigating Africa. Once I distanced myself from men and relegated their roles to temporary, contract work, the threats to my life and my property disappeared. Every Black American expat I knew who had been harmed in Africa had placed too much trust in men who eventually turned on them. By surrounding myself with women who had no desire to compete with me but instead wanted to build with me, I was able to survive in an environment where betrayal is common. This profound understanding—drawn from both human nature and the natural world—became the key to my survival. It's a model that others should take seriously when navigating this unpredictable landscape.

Wearing Poverty / My Armor in a Ruthless World

Another crucial survival tactic was the choice of apparel. With over 80 percent of the population living in visible poverty, I had to take extreme measures to blend into the environment and remain anonymous, especially in villages and shanty towns. I quickly observed the locals' attire and discarded my usual clothes. Instead, I adopted worn sandals, an old shirt, and simple shorts or sweatpants. The goal was to look like I didn't have much—just another face in the crowd, blending in with the local population and avoiding unwanted attention.

This strategy proved incredibly effective. People would often mock me, saying, "Look how you dress, you're not a true American," which sometimes stung. But I knew that if I was being made fun of for looking poor, then my tactic was working. Dressing down allowed me to move through these areas unnoticed and kept me safer in unpredictable situations. It was a small price to pay for protection in a place where standing out could cost you everything.

Assets Lossed

50 acres of prime roadside agricultural and development land

The 50 acres of land, all prime roadside property, were strategically positioned to meet logistical needs with ease. This ideal location made the land highly valuable for development and transportation access, offering immense potential for future ventures.

6 large-scale, high-yield farms

The six farms were situated on high-quality land, meticulously cultivated to produce agricultural products vital to the local food supply. Located near a major town, these farms played a crucial role in sustaining the surrounding communities.

Solar panel production and research center

The solar panel production and research center was housed in a large project facility, strategically located in a picturesque village setting. Even though this started out as my primary residence, the prime location, surrounded by abundant natural resources, provided the ideal environment to bring the ambitious project to life, fostering innovation and sustainable energy development.

Outdoor cinema

The outdoor cinema was more than just a place for films—it served as a venue for meetings, conventions, and cultural shows. Situated along the roadside near a university, it was the first of its kind in this region of Africa. Beyond the cinema, the property also featured a food court and a lounge, making it a vibrant hub for both entertainment and community gatherings.

Mount Collins Astronomy Zone

My first home in the village sat at the foot of a large mountain, which I transformed into an astronomy zone, inspired by the vast Zambian skies. Many local Zambians, fascinated by the stars and planets, took an interest in astronomy and worked alongside me to bring the project to life.

100+ mango trees along with dragon fruit, lemon, orange, avocado, and other exotic fruit trees.

The orchards included over 100 mango trees, along with exotic fruits like dragon fruit, lemon, orange, and avocado. These fruits weren't just for consumption—they were also used to produce sauces and juices, creating new revenue streams and positioning the orchards as an essential part of the local economy.

Exotic skins enterprise specializing in rare venomous snake skins

What began as a negative situation evolved into a thriving enterprise. Initially, I faced constant encounters with venomous snakes, and my first instinct was to have them killed, just as I saw men do every day. However, these snakes, though common here, were rare and highly prized around the world. That realization led me to explore the exotic skin business. I struck a deal with local snake hunters to supply the skins, and from there, the venture quickly took off. What was once a daily danger became the foundation of a unique and profitable enterprise.

During my time in Africa, I lost between $10 and $15 million in assets, not to mention the immense opportunity costs. These losses didn't happen overnight—they were the result of years of investment, effort, and dedication. Fifty acres of prime roadside land vanished. More than 100 mango and exotic fruit trees were burned to the ground. My outdoor cinema, once a vibrant hub for culture and community, was forfeited. Six high-yield farms, critical to the local food supply, were wiped out. These weren't just financial losses—they were the foundation of my vision, now reduced to ashes.

200 Years of Remminance

The losses I faced in Zambia made me realize something far more disturbing—if this is what one Black American experienced, imagine the devastation if we moved to Africa en masse. My research into history revealed that this wasn't a new story. In fact, it had happened before, several times over.

In the early 1900s, Chief Alfred Sam proposed a plan for Black Americans in Oklahoma to relocate to his homeland, Ghana. Desperate for a better life, many seized the opportunity, believing it was their path to a new beginning. But once they arrived, they quickly realized they had been duped. Everything they had worked for was lost in what turned out to be yet another elaborate scam, preying on the hope Black Americans carried for a fresh start in Africa. And this was far from the first time such exploitation had occurred.

A century earlier, in the 1820s, the American Colonization Society, with the backing of the U.S. government—including President James Monroe—launched an initiative to settle Black Americans in Africa, specifically in what would become Sierra Leone and Liberia. The project was fraught with difficulties, from deadly outbreaks of malaria on Sherbro Island to the resistance they faced from local Africans. When descendants of slaves finally settled in Cape Mesurado, Liberia, they were met with fierce resentment from local chiefs, who saw them as outsiders threatening their way of life. The Black American settlers, who sought to abolish the slave trade in the region, found themselves in violent clashes with local African leaders like Zolu Dum, who fought to preserve the very trade Black Americans had escaped.

But perhaps the most telling case for me was the work of William Nesbit in the 1850s. He traveled to Liberia to investigate the American Colonization Society's agenda of resettling Black Americans in Africa instead of granting them full citizenship in the U.S. Nesbit exposed the society for what it truly was: a Trojan horse designed to lure Black Americans to Africa, where death, disease, and exploitation awaited them. The colonizers knew how deadly Africa could be, and rather than see Black Americans gain equality in the U.S., they dangled the false hope of a new life on African soil.

This memoir draws inspiration from Nesbit's work, as the patterns I observed echo his findings. Over 200 years of historical evidence point to the same unsettling truth: Africa has been a land of betrayal for Black Americans. From the failed back-to-Africa movements to the violent resistance Black Americans faced from local Africans—whether for opposing the slave trade in the 1800s or for leading political movements like the George Floyd uprisings—African hostility toward Black Americans has deep roots and continues to surface. The remnants of this resentment are clear, whether in the past or now, as Africans repeatedly resist Black Americans' efforts to bring about progress or unity.

White supremacy has long understood and weaponized this divide. While Black Americans face hell in the U.S., we remain resilient and nearly impossible to defeat on our own soil. But if we place our lives and futures in the hands of Africa and its people, we risk our ultimate downfall. The hard truth is this: Africa is not our ally, and the dream of Pan-African unity is nothing more than a myth. If Black Americans seek salvation in Africa, we may very well meet our final demise.

Though my journey was tragic, the mission was ultimately accomplished. The goal was to determine if Black Americans could truly settle and thrive in Africa in modern times, and through my own trials, I uncovered the painful truth: Pan-Africanism, as we imagine it, doesn't exist outside of Black American idealism. It's not just Ghana— there's only one Africa, and the mindset is virtually the same across the continent. Just as Nesbit exposed the death trap of the American Colonization Society, I'm glad to have revealed the trojan horse in Ghana's "Year of Return." The lessons I've learned serve as a critical warning to those dreaming of refuge on the African continent— reminding us that the future lies not in romanticized reunification, but in understanding and embracing our strength here at home.

Last Statement

To the Black Americans who left everything behind in pursuit of a dream in Africa—those who braved the journey across the Atlantic, tired of the relentless grip of white supremacy—you are the embodiment of resilience and courage. Your move was nothing short of daring, an act that defied the odds and showed a spirit hungry for change. While 90% of the world clings to the American dream, you saw through the illusion. You sought something greater, something more meaningful. Your choice to embrace Africa as a Black person speaks volumes about your commitment to the Black race and your desire to build a better future. You are, without question, on the right side of history. Even if you lost possessions, faced hardships, or endured painful experiences, never forget this:

You didn't fail—Africa failed you.

www.ingramcontent.com/pod-product-compliance
Lightning Source LLC
Chambersburg PA
CBHW081533120626
46550CB00009B/2712